MEANINGFUL INVOLVEMENT AND FAIR TREATMENT BY TRIBAL ENVIRONMENTAL REGULATORY PROGRAMS

A Report of the
NATIONAL ENVIRONMENTAL JUSTICE ADVISORY COUNCIL

Prepared by
The National Environmental Justice Advisory Council
Indigenous Peoples Subcommittee

NATIONAL ENVIRONMENTAL JUSTICE ADVISORY COUNCIL

Indigenous Peoples Subcommittee (IPS) Members:

Terry Williams, The Tulalip Tribes Fisheries & Natural Resources, Maryville, Washington Chair)
Charon Asetoyer, Honor the Earth, Lake Andes, South Dakota
Chris Peters, Seventh Generation Fund, Arcata, California
Coleen Poler, Sokaogon Defense Committee, Crandon, Wisconsin
Karen Wilde Rogers, Colorado Commission of Indian Affairs, Denver, Colorado
Calvert Curley, Navajo Nation Environmental Protection Agency, Window Rock, Arizona
Pemina Yellow Bird, North Dakota Intertribal Reinterment Committee, Belcourt, North Dakota
Doo Jung Jin, Northwest College, Kirkland, Washington
John Roanhorse, Institute for Tribal Environmental Professionals, Tucson, Arizona

Designated Federal Officers*:

Daniel Gogal, Designated Federal Officer, Office of Environmental Justice, USEPA
Bob Smith, Alternate Designated Federal Officer, American Indian Environmental Office, USEPA

Technical Advisor and Consultant:

Tom Goldtooth, Technical Advisor, Indigenous Environmental Network, Bemjidi, Minnesota
Jeanette Wolfley, Esq., Attorney/Consultant, Pocatello, Idaho

*   *The Designated Federal Officer and Alternate Designated Federal Officer are not members of the Subcommittee, but are responsible for providing assistance to the Subcommittee in their efforts to be responsive to the Agency's request for advice and recommendations. This document was developed in direct response to the EPA's Office of Environmental Justice request for advice and recommendations on meaningful involvement and fair treatment by tribal environmental regulatory programs.*

This report and recommendations have been written as part of the activities of the National Environmental Justice Advisory Council (NEJAC), a public federal advisory committee providing independent advice and recommendations on the issue of environmental justice to the Administrator and other officials of the U.S. Environmental Protection Agency (EPA).

This report has not been reviewed or approved by the EPA. Therefore, its contents and recommendations do not represent the views and the policies of EPA or of any other agency of the federal government.

November 15, 2004

Administrator Michael Leavitt
U.S. Environmental Protection Agency
1200 Pennsylvania Avenue, NW
Washington, DC 20460

Dear Administrator Leavitt:

We are pleased to provide you a copy of the National Environmental Justice Advisory Council's report entitled **"Meaningful Involvement and Fair Treatment by Tribal Environmental Regulatory Programs,** dated November 2004" This document is intended to stimulate thought, discussion, and action to enhance environmental justice for indigenous peoples and others living and working in Indian country and in Alaska Native villages. This report builds on a document created by the NEJAC in November 2000, **"Guide on Consultation and Collaboration with Indian Tribal Governments and the Public Participation of Indigenous Groups and Tribal Members in Environmental Decision Making,"** which focuses on how EPA can more effectively consult and collaborate with tribes to address the range of environmental and public health issues in Indian country and of concern to tribes. This recent report discusses EPA's role in helping tribes develop processes for effective public participation and due process, as they develop and implement federally-approved environmental programs. To enhance the effectiveness of the report and recognition of tribal sovereignty, the IPS's "Preliminary Working Draft" of the report was mailed to each tribe in late February for review and comments. Those who commented received a copy of the "Revised Draft" in early August for additional review and comments.

This report proposes several overarching consensus recommendations to the EPA and other federal agencies. The following are the report's seven main recommendations:

1.   EPA should work with tribes to develop an understanding of tribal traditional principles of equity, fairness, and justice so to better understand the tribes' due process and public participation approaches.

2.   EPA should develop materials to inform tribal governments about the federal environmental laws and regulations requiring public participation and due process.

3.   EPA should work collaboratively with tribes to develop training and education for tribes, tribal members, and tribal community-based organizations on meaningful involvement and fair treatment.

4.   EPA should assist the tribes who are interested in developing administrative procedures (including processes for public participation and due process) so they will be better prepared to develop and implement federally-approved tribal environmental programs.

5. EPA should support coordination and collaboration among the tribes that have established meaningful involvement and fair treatment processes with the tribes seeking to develop their own processes.

6. EPA should help the tribes interested in fostering a dialogue with business and industry, states, local governments, and non-members on the issues of sovereignty, jurisdiction, and land ownership, which are likely to arise in the development and implementation of meaningful involvement and fair treatment processes.

7. EPA should recognize the unique situation of Alaska Natives with respect to the implementation of federal environmental laws in Alaska, and develop a better understanding of how to work with Alaska Native Tribes to address the multiplicity of environmental issues they face, including meaningful involvement and fair treatment in the development and implementation of federal environmental laws by EPA and the State of Alaska, and the State's environmental laws.

I thank you for your consideration of the advice and recommendations presented in this report, and look forward to discussing the important points raised in this document with the appropriate staff at EPA.

Sincerely,

Veronica Eady /s/   *Terry Williams* /s/

Veronica Eady, Chair   Terry Williams, Chair
National Environmental Justice Advisory Council   Indigenous Peoples Subcommittee

Enclosure

TABLE OF CONTENTS

EXECUTIVE SUMMARY   i

CHAPTER 1
I.   Background, Purpose and Summary   1
        NEJAC's Advice   4

CHAPTER 2
II.   Defining "Meaningful Involvement" and "Fair Treatment"   5
        A.   Tribal Definitions of Fairness and/or Due Process   6
        B.   Other Sources of Definitions of Due Process and Public
                Participation   7
                1.   Indian Civil Rights Act   8
                2.   International Human Rights   9
                3.   Federal Laws on Human Rights   10
                4.   Federal Environmental Laws   11
                        a.   Public Participation Under the Clean Water Act,
                                the Safe Drinking Water Act, and the Clean
                                Air Act   11
                        b.   The National Environmental Policy Act   12
                5.   EPA Public Involvement Policy   13
        NEJAC's Advice and Recommendations   15

CHAPTER 3
III.   Providing Public Participation and Due Process   17
        A.   Administrative Law Principles in Environmental Programs   17
                1.   Public Participation in Rulemaking   18
                2.   Due Process in Adjudication   19
        B.   Other Measures to Ensure Meaningful Public Participation   22
        C.   Tribal Models Effectively Providing Meaningful Public
                Participation and Fair Treatment   24
        D.   EPA's Role in Meeting the Charge   26
        NEJAC's Advice and Recommendations   28

CONCLUSION   31

ENDNOTES   33

APPENDICES
        A.   NEJAC/Indigenous Peoples Subcommittee Tribal Environmental
                Justice Charge   A-1
        B.   Significant Federal Policies Impacting Tribal Government   B-1
        C.   Providing for Meaningful Involvement and Fair Treatment   C-1
        D.   Glossary   D-1

EXECUTIVE SUMMARY

The National Environmental Justice Advisory Council (NEJAC) is presenting this report in response to EPA's request for advice and recommendations on meaningful involvement and fair treatment by tribal environmental regulatory programs. The report, prepared by the NEJAC's Indigenous Peoples' Subcommittee (IPS), specifically responds to the EPA's Charge, for advice and recommendations on the following questions:

> *In what ways should EPA assist Tribal governments to provide meaningful public involvement in the development and implementation of federally authorized and/or approved tribal environmental programs?*

> *In what ways should EPA assist Tribal governments to provide fair treatment of all stakeholders in the development and implementation of federally authorized and/or approved tribal environmental programs?*

The NEJAC is the formal federal advisory committee chartered, pursuant to the Federal Advisory Committee Act, to provide advice and recommendations to the Administrator of the U.S. Environmental Protection Agency (EPA) on matters related to environmental justice. The IPS consists of representatives from tribal governments, indigenous grassroots groups, environmental organizations, business and industry, academia, and state government.

The issues of meaningful involvement and due process, as they apply to tribal governments, are inherently complex and may be difficult to resolve. The NEJAC acknowledges that tribes are at different stages in the development of their environmental programs, and are employing different approaches based on their particular culture, history, government structure, and land base. It is important that EPA recognizes, and is sensitive to, American Indian and Alaska Native tribal concerns about sovereignty and tribal decision-making processes. In other words, EPA must be mindful of the unique cultures, traditions and government structures of each tribe.

Additionally, the NEJAC stresses that the examination of public participation and due process within the tribal context should not be limited to a comparison with state and federal due process procedures. There must be an understanding of, or reference to, the tribal values of due process and public participation within in the tribal culture and context. To that end, a tribal institution, albeit a tribal court, administrative body, or dispute resolution committee, must be given the opportunity to articulate the tribal cultural and social norms of public participation and fair treatment. It is through this process that tribes can best preserve, strengthen and incorporate native concepts of equity and justice, and build communication and cooperation within the communities they serve.

The NEJAC has documented numerous examples of tribes that have already defined for themselves "due process" and "public participation". These definitions are articulated in tribal oral traditions, and in written tribal constitutions, bill of rights laws, tribal civil rights acts, tribal court decisions and policies. In addition to tribal definitions, there are other sources of law that define due process and meaningful involvement including the American Indian Civil Rights Act of 1968, the International Human Rights covenants, the federal laws on human rights such as the Indian Religious Freedom Act and Native American Graves Protection and Repatriation Act, the various federal environmental laws and EPA's public involvement policy. Tribes may choose to use these other sources in their public participation and meaningful involvement efforts.

The NEJAC further provides some examples of processes and procedures tribes have established and are utilizing to ensure meaningful involvement and due process are afforded to tribal members and non-members. Several tribes have chosen to incorporate their decision-making processes and actions into their administrative procedures, in accordance with administrative law. Administrative law procedures are accepted and established processes that provide fundamental fairness, meaningful public participation, and greater certainty and predictability for implementation of tribal environmental laws. Additionally, there are other tribes who have developed processes, oral and written, for addressing fair treatment and public participation. Three examples are provided from Alaska, Washington and Idaho.

The NEJAC believes that any EPA proposal that truly values the extension, or enhancement, of meaningful involvement and fair treatment in Indian country and in Alaska Native villages must recognize the need for financial resources to support tribal environmental programs, and training and education for tribes on meaningful involvement and fair treatment. The NEJAC has provided several recommendations regarding training, education and funding.

The NEJAC has proposed 7 specific points of advice and 14 recommendations in this report. These are both general and specific in nature, some interrelated, and are provided in the spirit of seeking to identify all possible issues, alternatives and approaches to the issues presented in the Charge. The advice and recommendations follow each chapter. Finally, there are two main appendices (B and C) that are important background documents for readers to consider in conjunction with the main report.

MEANINGFUL INVOLVEMENT AND FAIR TREATMENT BY TRIBAL ENVIRONMENTAL REGULATORY PROGRAMS

CHAPTER 1

I. Background, Purpose and Summary

The National Environmental Justice Advisory Council (NEJAC) is the formal federal advisory committee chartered, pursuant to the Federal Advisory Committee Act, to provide advice and recommendations to the Administrator of the U.S. Environmental Protection Agency (EPA) on matters related to environmental justice. The NEJAC is presenting this report in response to EPA's request for advice and recommendations on meaningful involvement and fair treatment by tribal environmental regulatory programs. The report, prepared by the NEJAC's Indigenous Peoples' Subcommittee (IPS) and reviewed and approved, with changes, by the NEJAC Executive Council, specifically responds to the EPA's Charge, for advice and recommendations on the following questions:

> *In what ways should EPA assist Tribal governments to provide meaningful public involvement in the development and implementation of federally authorized and/or approved tribal environmental programs?*

> *In what ways should EPA assist Tribal governments to provide fair treatment of all stakeholders in the development and implementation of federally authorized and/or approved tribal environmental programs?*

A. Background

The Indigenous Peoples Subcommittee (IPS) is one of seven subcommittees of the National Environmental Justice Advisory Council (NEJAC). The IPS assists the NEJAC in providing advice and recommendations on how the Agency can most effectively address environmental justice issues/concerns facing federally-recognized tribes and other indigenous peoples. The IPS has eight members with diverse backgrounds who represent tribal governments, indigenous grassroots groups, environmental organizations, business and industry, academia and state government.

Over the past 20 years, tribes throughout the United States have begun to develop and implement tribal environmental programs, pursuant to amendments in federal statutes and regulations, which provide that tribes can assume roles similar to states. In order to protect human health and environmental and cultural integrity on their reservations, many tribes are in the process of defining their tribal authority. Tribes have begun planning and developing the basic frameworks and institutions for protecting air quality, preserving water quality, and managing contamination and pollution caused by solid and hazardous wastes. Under the various federal environmental laws, the EPA approves, and tribes receive, federal authority to regulate and set standards on reservations to protect human health and the environment.

Tribal regulatory authority, in the environmental arena, has been challenged by non-member and non-Indian residents of the tribal community or reservation. The challengers maintain that the tribal governments do not possess civil jurisdiction to regulate their activities on the reservation, and argue that tribes do not provide public participation avenues and due process. Thus far, tribal governments have successfully overcome the challenges to their regulatory authority. These challenges, however, raise a host of ongoing legal, social, community and political issues. Indeed, the Congress has held oversight hearings on the civil jurisdiction of tribal governments and tribal sovereignty.

B.   Purpose

In the context of these experiences and in the EPA approval process of tribal environmental programs, the EPA, through its Office of Environmental Justice, issued a Charge to the NEJAC to provide advice and recommendations on the issues of public participation and due process as these principles relate to federally-authorized tribal environmental regulatory programs.[1] The NEJAC tasked its Indigenous People's Subcommittee (Appendix A) to prepare this report, which was reviewed and approved, with changes, by the NEJAC Executive Council which respectfully submits it in response to the EPA's Charge. The NEJAC emphasizes that the Charge, and the discussion in this document, applies only to federally-funded or EPA-approved tribal environmental programs. However, some tribes who rely solely upon their inherent sovereign powers for environmental management may find the advice, recommendations, and tribal examples in this report useful for their consideration.

C.   Summary

This report seeks to address the EPA's questions in the Charge and is intended to encourage a candid discussion, as well as to stimulate thought and action about the issue of meaningful involvement and fair treatment by tribal governments. Tribes are at different stages in the development of their environmental programs, and are employing different approaches to environmental management based on their culture, history, government structure, and land base. As discussed in this report, some tribes currently employ the principles of public involvement and fair treatment for tribal and non-member residents of the tribal community. The application of such basic human principles promises to strengthen and better articulate tribal sovereignty.

The NEJAC stresses that the discussion of public participation and application of due process principles to tribal governments, however, must be cognizant of the unique culture, traditions and government structure of each tribe. There are over 560 tribes in the United States, and they are different from one another. The ability to realize due process principles requires more than tribes simply adopting European-style procedures. In other words, the examination of due process and public participation within the tribal context should not be limited to a comparison with state and federal due process procedures. There must be an understanding of, or reference to, the tribal values of due process within the tribal culture and context. A tribal institution- through a rulemaking or review by a tribal administrative agency, dispute resolution board, or tribal court- must be given the opportunity to articulate the cultural and social norms of due process. It is through the tribal process that tribes can best preserve, strengthen and incorporate native concepts of equity and justice, and build communication, cooperation and support within the tribal community. This represents tribal sovereignty in action.

Additionally, the NEJAC acknowledges that, for some tribes, there must be a tribal political commitment to build institutional capability. This is necessary to make meaningful public participation and fair treatment possible and can be accomplished with funding assistance and technical advice from the EPA. Simply stated, developing meaningful involvement and fair treatment processes within a tribal setting cannot be an end in itself. Tribes can and should consider approaches to improve the process, which can help enhance community respect for tribal procedures. It is through institution-building and community support that tribes can provide for effective public participation and fair treatment.

In the view of the NEJAC, it is critical to provide adequate financial resources to support the tribes' environmental programs, as well as the development and implementation of public participation and fair treatment processes. Moreover, any EPA proposal, which truly values the extension of due process to tribal members and the public, must recognize the need for tribes to receive training and education in the areas of public participation and due process. Training can serve as a two-way exchange; tribes can learn about the principles of non-tribal public participation and due process while EPA, as well as the non-member residents and other interested parties, can learn about tribal processes of participation and equity. In the absence of such financial and technical resources/training, meaningful public participation and fair treatment may not be realized.

The NEJAC recognizes that any discussion regarding public participation and due process by tribal environmental regulatory programs is complex and may be difficult to resolve. From the outset, it is important that EPA recognizes and is sensitive to tribal government concerns about encroachment upon their tribal decision-making and sovereignty in developing environmental programs based upon their traditions and governmental structure. Indeed, some tribes may believe that EPA has singled out tribes on the issues addressed in this document.

Finally, the NEJAC observes that tribal members, as well as reservation and Alaska Native lands, have suffered disproportionate environmental impacts. They are often overburdened, underserved, underfunded, and suffer high risks from environmental impacts which affect public health. It is important that EPA acknowledge that some tribal governments are focused on the basic governmental services of education, affordable housing, food and nutrition, clean water, and reducing exposure to contaminants. These basic services are critical priorities to many American Indian and Alaska Native communities and often overshadow the public participation ideals and values articulated by EPA in its Charge. The NEJAC notes the existence of these fundamental and ever-pressing issues and recognizes that they may limit tribal attention to public involvement issues. Accordingly, EPA should proceed with great sensitivity in dealing with tribal governments on the issues of due process and public participation.

This report begins in Chapter 2 with a presentation of established tribal definitions of due process, and other sources for defining due process under the Indian Civil Rights Act, international human rights law, and federal environmental laws. Chapter 3 discusses current tribal procedures or processes to ensure public participation and due process.

At the end of each chapter, the NEJAC presents advice and recommendations on ways in which the EPA can assist tribes in addressing, developing and implementing meaningful involvement and fair treatment processes. Chapter 3 includes advice and recommendations compiled from Appendices B and C. The advice and recommendations are both general and specific, and are provided in the spirit of seeking to identify possible approaches to addressing the issues raised in the Charge.

D.   Appendices

The report contains a set of three appendices that include: (1) the NEJAC Charge (Appendix A); (2) a discussion of the significant federal policies impacting tribal governments and the authority or sovereignty of tribes to protect and regulate activities affecting natural resources and the environment of reservations (Appendix B); and (3) the terms of "meaningful public involvement" and "due process", and why these principles are important for tribes and governments in general to consider (Appendix C).

NEJAC's Advice and Recommendation

Advice

1.1   EPA should recognize that requirements for public participation and due process in federally-approved tribal environmental programs may have implications for tribal decision making, values, sovereignty, and tribal efforts to exert jurisdictional authority. EPA should be sensitive to these concerns and to the challenges these bring to tribes.

1.2   EPA should continue to enhance its government-to-government consultation and collaboration with tribes, as tribes exercise their sovereignty, exert jurisdiction over environmental and public health issues, and develop and implement tribal environmental programs.

CHAPTER 2

II.   Defining "Meaningful Involvement" and "Fair Treatment"[2]

In defining these terms for tribes, some may be naturally inclined to borrow familiar principles from the areas of federal constitutional, statutory law or policies. For example, the EPA has defined these phrases in their Environmental Justice Policy. In 1992, EPA created the Office of Environmental Justice to integrate environmental justice into the Agency's policies, programs, and activities. EPA defines "environmental justice" as the "fair treatment and meaningful involvement of all people regardless of race, color, national origin, or income with respect to the development, implementation, and enforcement of environmental laws, regulations, and policies."[3] EPA further defines the terms "meaningful involvement" and "fair treatment" as follows:

> **Meaningful involvement** means that: (1) potentially affected community residents have an appropriate opportunity to participate in decisions about a proposed activity that will affect their environment and/or health; (2) the public contribution can influence the regulatory agency's decision; (3) the concerns of all participants involved will be considered in the decision making process; and (4) the decision makers seek out and facilitate the involvement of those potentially affected.[4]

> **Fair treatment** means that no group of people, including racial, ethnic, or socioeconomic group should bear a disproportionate share of the negative environmental consequences resulting from industrial, municipal, and commercial operations or the execution of federal, state, local and tribal programs or policies.

The NEJAC notes that direct application of due process principles developed by federal or state courts may be inappropriate for tribal communities because such standards or principles are designed to protect the interests of individuals in the majority society and often do not reflect the unique communal interests of tribes. Identifying the best interests of tribal nations and their people presents a weighty challenge for tribal governments. Ultimately, each tribe must define for itself the process best suited for their needs. It is quite probable that tribes may exhibit a combination of borrowed principles and traditional tribal principles. The various forms of public participation that may be adopted or created by tribal governments are virtually endless.

The NEJAC has identified numerous instances where tribes have defined "due process" and "meaningful involvement" within their communities based upon traditional tribal principles. These are illustrated in tribal court decisions, constitutions, codes, and policies. Other sources, such as the Indian Civil Rights Act and judicial interpretations, International Human Rights documents, federal human rights legislation, and federal environmental laws and regulations are presented as well. These additional sources may provide insight and be of use to EPA as the Agency works with tribes to provide for meaningful involvement and due process in tribal environmental regulatory programs.

A.   Tribal Definitions of Fairness and/or Due Process

Fairness, or due process, is not new to tribal governments. Indeed, Chief Justice Sherman, Rosebud Sioux Tribal Court, stated in <u>Bloomberg</u> v. <u>Dreamer</u> (1991):

> It should not be for the Congress of the United States or the Federal Court of Appeals to tell us when to give due process. Due process is a concept that has always been with us. Although it is a legal phrase and has legal meaning, due process means nothing more than being fair and honest in our dealings with each other. We are allowed to disagree...What must be remembered is that we must allow the other side the opportunity to be heard.[5]

Similarly, the Navajo Supreme Court has noted that Navajo customary due process predates the Indian Civil Rights Act and the Navajo Bill of Rights. The Court described Navajo due process as a form of dispute resolution, where all interested parties get a chance to speak before a collective decision is made.[6] Tribal common law, as developed by the tribal judiciary, is a good source for defining due process. Furthermore, tribal judges are tribal leaders who must make day-to-day decisions for the good of the whole community, while simultaneously maintaining the integrity of the case for those individuals before him or her. Restorative justice, practiced by the Navajo Peacemaker Court and other similar tribal forums, advocates balance and harmony between the parties and for the overall good of the tribal community.

Many tribal constitutions include measures to provide for a good quality of life for the people and to protect the health, security and general welfare of the tribes through mechanisms of fairness and due process. For example, the Constitution of the Spokane Tribe of Indians provides:

> ... [t]his Constitution and the Tribal Government it establishes shall not encroach upon or limit any person's right to enjoy freedom of worship, conscience, speech, press, assembly and association, and other rights established by federal law.[7]

Similarly, Article X of the Rosebud Sioux Tribe Constitution establishes a Bill of Rights:

> No person shall be...deprived of life, liberty, or property, without due process of law; not be denied equal protection of law.[8]

Some tribes have enacted civil rights ordinances, which similarly provide mandatory due process. The Confederated Tribes of the Colville Reservation have adopted such an ordinance. Chapter 1-5-2(h) Colville Tribal Civil Rights Act states that the Tribal government:

> "…shall not deny to any person within its jurisdiction the equal protection of its laws or deprive any person of liberty or property without due process of law."[9]

Other tribes have administrative procedure acts to establish notice, comment procedures and due process.[10]

Fair dealings, honesty, integrity, and the opportunity to be heard or speak before a collective decision is made, are all worthy and tribally-recognized components of due process. These universal understandings of fairness, through tribal customs and traditions, have been handed down by word of mouth or by example from one generation to another without any written instruction or mandate. These long established practices are considered unwritten law and reflect a tribal community's practices that regulate social life.

Today, many tribal constitutions and law and order codes provide for due process and public participation, as the examples above demonstrate. These provisions mandate that custom and tradition be utilized by tribal courts and other dispute resolution processes. Many tribal institutions apply and draw upon customary law to some extent. Applying customary law is not always simple because the customs are often contained in the oral traditions of tribes.[11] They are not written down or codified like state or federal standards. Instead, the sources of common law are the members of the tribe who retain the traditions of the tribe. However, this does not mean that tribal standards of due process should be disregarded simply because they are not written. Tribal definitions of due process can be adopted by tribal environmental programs and incorporated into their procedures by working with individual community representatives who can assist in the articulation of the due process within the local tribal context.

In recent years, tribes have begun to reexamine their current tribal justice practices and standards of justice, and are revitalizing and re-traditionalizing their justice systems. They are exploring the old unwritten law of the past as a means to restore their tribal culture and health of the tribal community. The area of customary law, including methods of traditional dispute resolution, is receiving attention from legal experts and researchers. Customary law and the articulation of tribal standards, definitions and principles relating to fairness, thoughtful deliberation, honesty, the opportunity to speak before a collective decision is made, respect for each other, and harmony and balance with the community should be recognized and given due consideration by tribal environmental programs when they begin to consider and articulate public participation and fair treatment policies.

B.   Other Sources of Definitions of Due Process and Public Participation

In addition to tribal legal definitions, there are other sources of law defining due process and public involvement.

1. Indian Civil Rights Act

In 1968, Congress enacted the Indian Civil Rights Act of 1968 (ICRA).[12] Widely called the "Indian Bill of Rights," this document was used by Congress to impose certain limitations on tribes, closely resembling provisions of the U.S. Constitution's First, Fourth, Fifth, Sixth, and Eighth Amendments and the equal protection and due process provisions of the Fourteenth Amendment. Section 1302(8) of the ICRA provides that: "No tribe in exercising powers of self-government shall . . . deny to any person within its jurisdiction the equal protection of its laws or deprive any person of liberty or property without due process of law." The act applies to tribal action against all individuals, both tribal members and non-members.[13]

Some tribes have incorporated the ICRA into their constitutions or tribal codes, while others include the Bill of Rights provisions in their constitutions. For example, the Jamestown S'Klallam Tribe of Indians in Washington, adopted ICRA provisions verbatim into their Tribal Constitution.[14] Another Washington tribe, the Skokomish Indian Tribe, has paraphrased the ICRA provisions in their Constitution and added that the Tribe:

> "…shall provide to all persons within its jurisdiction the rights guaranteed by the Indian Civil Rights Act of 1968."[15]

Under the ICRA, tribal courts or forums review and interpret tribal law and actions to determine if there is a violation of certain individual rights, such as due process. In 1978, in the landmark case of *Santa Clara Pueblo v. Martinez*, the Supreme Court held that Section 1303 of the ICRA is the exclusive federal remedy (*habeas corpus*) under the statute. This means that virtually all ICRA litigation proceeds through the tribal judicial systems, and federal courts rarely hear Indian civil rights cases.[16]

Accordingly, tribal courts have had the opportunity to define due process under the ICRA involving a variety of issues. Tribal courts have looked to federal precedent and tribal traditions to discern the essential fairness implied by the requirement of due process. Many tribal courts have held that tribes have greater flexibility in applying principles of due process as found in the ICRA, than state and federal courts have in applying principles of due process under their respective constitutions.[17] Moreover, the tribal courts routinely rule that the meaning and application of the ICRA is not determined by European-style constitutional interpretations.[18] Importantly, the rights of individuals often are balanced against the communal good of the tribe.

Some federal courts, which faced claims of due process violations by tribes, have found that a ten-day notice and opportunity to speak before a tribal council met the requirements of due process.[19] In addition, the courts have found that the failure of a tribal chairman to present his side of the case in the traditional tribal forum – a tribal council – did not constitute a violation of due process.[20] However, a federal court found a violation of due process when a tribal member was not given a meaningful opportunity to be heard,[21] and when a tribe imposed permanent orders of banishment without a hearing or prior notice.[22]

It is clear from a review of the case law that tribal courts are making a good faith interpretation of the ICRA. The substantive holdings of the cases protect individual rights and contemplate unique tribal customs and traditions. Promoting tribal sovereignty begins with tribal courts applying tribal law to settle tribal member and tribal government disputes. Recognition of these principles of due process under the ICRA provides a foundation for such application in the environmental regulatory setting, and should be used as a guide for implementing tribal environmental acts and regulations. Common due process principles, such as a notice of a hearing, a forum or body to hear complaints or permits, the opportunity to be heard, and the right to an appeal of a decision have been upheld by the tribal courts and federal courts in interpreting the ICRA. These basic principles should also apply to tribal environmental programs when they implement their rules and regulations.

2.   International Human Rights

The International Covenant on Civil and Political Rights;[23] the International Covenant on Economic, Social and Cultural Rights and the Draft American Declaration on the Rights of Indigenous Peoples are important international sources of human rights law for American Indians, Alaska Natives, Native Hawaiians, and tribal governments. The first two documents transform the value embodied in the Universal Declaration of Human Rights[24] into binding legal norms or standards. Together these instruments form the basis of contemporary human rights law. The first article of the two earliest covenants secures the right to self-determination for all peoples, indicating the primary importance of this right in international law:

> "All peoples have the right to self-determination. By virtue of that
> right they freely determine their political status and freely pursue
> their economic, social and cultural development."

Importantly, these international documents recognize the basic roots of sovereignty, that is, governments derive:

> "...their just powers from the consent of the governed," and the
> "collective rights of indigenous peoples" to possess and exercise
> rights.[25]

Three articles (14, 25, and 26) of the Covenant on Civil and Political Rights are relevant to the issue of due process and the provision of basic human rights to all people within the jurisdiction of a tribe. Article 14 proclaims that "[a]ll persons shall be equal before the courts and tribunals" and that any person's rights and obligations are to be determined in a "suit of law... shall be entitled to a fair and public hearing by an independent and impartial tribunal established by law." Article 25 provides that "[e]very citizen shall have the right and the opportunity ... without unreasonable restrictions to take part in the conduct of public affairs, directly or through freely chosen representatives." Certainly, non-members are not "citizens" of the tribe, but this provision aptly applies to tribal members who believe that their rights have been restricted or access not readily available to participate in tribal government hearings and meetings. Finally, Article 26, like the ICRA, provides: "All persons [tribal members or non-members] are equal before the law and are entitled without any discrimination to the equal protection of the law."

The most recent relevant international document is the Draft American Declaration on the Rights of Indigenous Peoples,[26] prepared by the Inter-American Commission on Human Rights in 1997. The Draft American Declaration contains important provisions for recognizing the collective rights of indigenous peoples and tribes, including right to lands and cultural rights. Importantly, the draft provides that indigenous peoples of the Americas have the "right to the full and effective enjoyment of the human rights and fundamental freedoms."[27] Article 13 of the draft establishes rights to environmental protection including:

> The right to a safe and healthy environment, which is an essential condition for the enjoyment of the right to life and collective well-being, to be informed of measures which will affect their environment, including information that ensures their effective participation in action and policies that may affect it, and to participate fully in formulating, planning, managing and applying governmental programmes of conservation of their lands, territories and resources.[28]

And, Article 18 recognizes the rights of landowners to their property and ownership rights with respect to their lands:

> The right to protection of their rights with respect to the natural resources on their lands, including the ability to use, manage, and conserve such resources; and with respect to traditional uses of their lands, interests in lands, and resources, such as subsistence."[29]

Significantly, the article provides that the

> "governments must establish or maintain procedures for the participation of the peoples concerned in determining whether the interests of these people would be adversely affected and to what extent, before undertaking or authorizing any program for planning, prospecting, or exploiting existing resources on their lands."[30]

3.   Federal Laws on Human Rights

As noted above, indigenous groups from the Americas, Australia, Africa and other parts of the World have joined in efforts to forge the protection of their rights on the basis of international law. Some of these international principles with regard to basic human rights, cultural freedoms and collective rights, may prove useful for tribal consideration when deliberating the concepts of meaningful public participation and fair treatment for their communities.

In the United States, the Congress has recognized the unique cultural need of tribes and enacted several pieces of legislation for the protection of tribal cultural properties and religious rights including the American Indian Religious Freedom Act[31], and the Native American Graves Protection and Repatriation Act.[32] Although these federal laws apply to federal land managers, tribes may wish to consider the values and principles articulated in these laws as they may apply to tribal government initiatives. These laws are based in part on basic human rights principles that seek to protect and preserve the cultural properties and religious beliefs of tribes. They formally acknowledge that the cultures of tribes are a vital part of the ongoing lifeways of the United States, and as such must be respected and are vital to the future of such peoples. Additionally, the legislation recognizes the cultural ties that tribes continue to have to the Earth and natural resources.

4.   Federal Environmental Laws

a.   Public Participation Under the Clean Water Act, the Safe Drinking Water Act, and the Clean Air Act

Tribes who have received federal authority, under "treatment as a state" provisions of the various federal environmental acts, should be keenly aware of the federal requirements for public participation set forth in the federal regulations. Part 25 of Title 40 of the Code of Federal Regulations governs public participation in programs under three of the primary laws administered by EPA: the Clean Water Act, the Safe Drinking Water Act and the Resource Conservation and Recovery Act.[33] Although Part 25 does not expressly apply to tribes, other EPA regulations make Part 25 applicable to tribes. For example, regulations under the Clean Water Act for water quality standards state that Part 25 regulations are applicable to states, and then to tribes when they seek treatment as a state and seek to adopt and review water quality standards.[34] The Clean Water Act authorizes EPA to treat tribes as states for a number of purposes under the federal statute, including section 303 for water quality standards, section 319 to control non-point sources of water pollution, section 401 for certification of compliance with water quality standards, section 402 for NPDES permits, and section 404 for dredging or filling wetlands. This means that tribal environmental programs must comply with these federal public participation regulations for rulemaking.

Part 25 regulations establish a host of requirements for sharing information, public notices and consultation.[35] Some of these requirements are:

> (1) A proactive program to provide information to the public, including making documents and summaries of complex documents available, establishing central and convenient collections points for documents, and maintaining an interested persons list for any activity covered by Part 25; (2) providing ample notice to all interested persons and affected parties, and making reports, documents and data available at least 30 days before a hearing; (3) the establishment of advisory groups, task

forces, and informal communication; and (4) preparation of responsiveness summaries by agencies to public comments.

If a tribe has enacted an administrative procedure act, the requirements of the tribal law should prevail if they conflict with the Part 25 requirements.

A second section of the Code of Federal Regulations that applies to tribes is Part 124. The procedures in Part 124 address permits issued by tribes who choose to be treated like states, under RCRA Subtitle C, the Safe Drinking Water Act underground injection control program, the Clean Air Act prevention of significant deterioration program and the NPDES program.[36] Part 124 set forth program requirements for draft permits, public notices, requests for hearings, final decisions and administrative appeals from decisions or orders, and judicial review of agency actions.[37]

In addition, under the Clean Air Act, Tribal Implementation Program (TIP) guideline, there are requirements that are consistent with 40 CFR Part 51.102(d), that cover notice to be given to the public for the proposed plan, time, date and place of the hearings, and making the proposed plan available for public inspection on and off the reservation and to ensure advertisement in a general circulation newspaper. Tribes have complied with this section in informing the public on their TIPs. The St. Regis Mohawk Tribe in New York published the notice in their local Tribal newspaper and circulated the information widely in the area. The Gila River Indian Community in Arizona published in a Phoenix newspaper and on the Reservation.

b. The National Environmental Policy Act

A significant federal law that establishes a comprehensive environment review of federal actions is the National Environmental Policy Act (NEPA).[38] Under NEPA, a federal agency may be required to prepare an environmental assessment or environmental impact statement prior to taking any "major federal action significantly affecting the quality of the human environment."[39] NEPA requires federal agencies to prepare documents analyzing the impacts and giving the public the right to participate in the process. In short, NEPA makes the federal decision making process a transparent one. Within the past 10 years, several tribes have initiated the adoption of NEPA-like review processes to consider the impacts of projects on public heath and safety, natural and cultural resources, socioeconomic conditions and the environment.[40] Some tribes have established laws in order to have a uniform permitting mechanism for on-reservation activities. These laws are referred to as "TEPAs" or Tribal Environmental Policy Acts.

As part of the review process, the TEPA provides for the reservation population, Indian and non-Indian to participate in the tribal decision making. There are established procedures that permit public participation and due process as the tribal government moves through its decision making process to consider a development project by the tribe itself or a private entity. For example, a tribe may establish a TEPA that has a permitting process that gives individuals the opportunity to express their concerns to the permitting agency on a housing or commercial development, and the applicant the opportunity to respond. Commonly, a TEPA has a process for administrative appeals and judicial review similar to the procedures discussed in Chapter 3 under the administrative law procedures section.   In addition, a tribe may craft a TEPA to include rulemaking under its coverage to enable the public to comment on and participate in the drafting of rules or regulations relating to the tribal clean air, water quality or solid waste laws.

Another important aspect of NEPA is the role and responsibilities of tribes and its members in the overall federal decision making process. Under the CEQ regulations, federal agencies are responsible for seeking the cooperation of state and Indian tribes if the proposed action may affect an Indian reservation, or impacts outside the reservation may affect cultural resources or off-reservation treaty rights.[41]   A tribe may become a cooperating agency, by agreement, which gives a tribe direct involvement in the key decisions and an opportunity to educate the agency about the tribal needs and concerns. If a tribe has a TEPA, the CEQ encourages the preparation of joint review documents and assessments, and to satisfy both the NEPA and TEPA requirements.

5.   EPA Public Involvement Policy

In May 2003, the EPA released its Public Involvement Policy to "provide for meaningful public involvement in all its programs, and consistently look for new ways to enhance public input."[42] The term "public involvement" is used in the Policy to "encompass the full range of actions and processes that EPA uses to engage the public in the Agency's work, and means that the Agency considers public concerns, values, and preferences when making decisions."[43] The Policy's purposes are to:

> Improve the acceptability, efficiency, feasibility and durability of the Agency's decisions; reaffirm EPA's commitment to early and meaningful public involvement; ensure that EPA makes its decisions considering the interests and concerns of affected people and entities; promote the use of a wide variety of techniques to create early and, when appropriate, continuing opportunities for public involvement in Agency decisions; and establish clear and effective guidance for conducting public involvement activities. [44]

EPA identified seven basic steps to ensure that it conducts effective meaningful public involvement:

> (1) plan and budget for public involvement activities;
> (2) identify the interested and affected public;
> (3) consider providing technical or financial assistance to the public to facilitate involvement;
> (4) provide information and outreach to the public;
> (5) conduct public consultation and involvement activities;
> (6) review and use input and provide feedback to the public; and
> (7) evaluate public involvement activities.[45]

The Policy includes a comprehensive guidance to help EPA staff and managers in implementing the seven steps.[46]

The Public Involvement Policy offers comprehensive creative methods, outreach efforts and alternative courses of action that can be utilized to inform the public about a wide variety of Agency proposed actions. The NEJAC recommends that EPA should encourage tribal environmental managers to review the Policy in order to gain insight and ideas that may be useful in their public participation efforts. Additionally, such measures enhance the deliberative process and promote a careful, critical examination of government decision-making.

Advice

2.1   EPA should recognize that tribes may use their oral traditions and customs to provide written standards of due process and meaningful involvement.

Recommendations

2.2   EPA should work with tribes to develop an understanding of tribal traditional principles of equity, fairness, and justice so to better understand the tribes' due process and public participation approaches.

2.3   EPA should work with tribes to inventory the definitions developed, and procedures used, by tribal courts and other tribal institutions for public participation and due process based upon tribal customary laws.

2.4   EPA should encourage federal agencies to collaborate with tribes, support tribal cooperating agency status in implementing the National Environmental Policy Act (NEPA) when actions may affect cultural resources and off-reservation treaty rights (on aboriginal, ceded, usual and accustomed lands), and build capacity for effective decision making, including meaningful involvement and fair treatment processes for NEPA implementation.

CHAPTER 3

III. Providing Public Participation and Due Process

In the preceding Chapter, this document discussed various definitions of due process and meaningful involvement, and provided examples of tribes who have defined the phrases within the tribal context. This Chapter further illustrates various processes, procedures and principles that tribes have established and are utilizing to ensure that meaningful public participation and due process are afforded to tribal members and other community members.

The NEJAC believes this information can assist tribes in their efforts to develop or enhance their own processes, since tribes can benefit from the successes of existing tribal programs. Section A explores the use of administrative law principles for addressing due process and meaningful involvement by tribal environmental programs. Section B discusses other measures for ensuring public participation. Section C includes additional examples of how tribes are providing for meaningful public involvement and fair treatment in the area of environmental protection. In Section D, the NEJAC discusses educational programs, and financial and technical support to aid tribes in developing and/or implementing meaningful public involvement and due process approaches in tribal environmental programs. The Chapter concludes with the NEJAC' Advice and Recommendations pertaining to this Chapter as well as those relevant to the information provided in the attached appendices.

A. Administrative Law Principles in Environmental Programs

To address the myriad of environmental issues and implementation of complex and highly specialized laws, tribal governments have established boards, departments, commissions and other administrative entities to oversee these programs. Some tribal environmental programs, as departments or agencies of a tribe, have chosen to incorporate their decision-making processes and actions into their administrative procedures, in accordance with administrative law.[47] Certainly, each tribe, in exercising their sovereignty, will determine what public participation processes and notions of due process are applicable to its community. Tribal administrative procedure laws, however, provide a guide for tribal administrative agencies to address permitting, enforcement and general rulemaking, which affect development and regulation of natural resources on Indian reservations. Administrative procedures are an accepted and established process that provides fundamental fairness, meaningful public participation, and greater certainty and predictability for the implementation of tribal environmental laws and regulatory programs.[48]

Administrative law is described as follows:

> Administrative law is the branch of the law that controls the administrative operations of government. Its primary purpose is to keep governmental powers within their legal bounds and to protect individuals against the abuse of such power. It sets forth the powers that may be exercised by administrative agencies, lays

down the principles governing the exercise of those powers, and provides legal remedies to those aggrieved by administrative action.[49]

Broadly speaking, administrative law covers three sets of issues: (1) delegation of powers by the legislative body to an administrative agency; (2) procedural and substantive limitations on the execution of the powers; and (3) procedural requirements and standards for administrative appeals and judicial review of administrative action. For purposes of this document, the two primary types of processes, "rulemaking" and "adjudication," may impact the interests and concerns of individuals, tribal members or non-members. These two processes have been adopted in administrative procedure acts by some tribal governments and are explored as approaches to ensure public participation and due process.

1.   **Public Participation in Rulemaking**

Rulemaking by a tribe is a legislative process that clarifies ambiguities or fills in gaps in the environmental ordinance or law that was passed by the tribal governing body. Usually, the governing body (typically the tribal council) has delegated the authority to draft and promulgate rules or regulations to the environmental program, and then the program undertakes this task to provide more details and specifics in the rules. For example, a tribal council may enact an air quality protection act and delegate authority to its air program to draft specific standards. The act itself is usually broader or more general in nature. For this reason, the air program staff will undertake rulemaking by drafting detailed rules or regulations defining air emission rates and setting emission limits, emission inventories, control measures and technologies for various sources, and compliance schedules, as well as others.

Generally, an environmental program or agency is accountable to the legislative body or tribal council, but not directly to the community or public. In order to provide public participation and allow federal agencies to be more accountable to the public, Congress has enacted the Administrative Procedures Act (APA).[50] Likewise, some tribes have enacted APAs to govern rulemaking for the tribal departments in general[51] and specifically to environmental programs. The tribal APAs establish procedural and substantive limitations on the exercise of tribal administrative authority, and typically establish notice, publication, and public comment procedures in connection with the adoption of rules or regulations (rulemaking). The acts also provide for public inspection of department decisions, orders, and opinions. For example, the Puyallup Tribal Administrative Procedure Act, Section 1.4, states:

> Prior to proposing that the Tribal Council adopt, amend or repeal any rule, the sponsoring Department proposing that the Tribal Council take such action shall:
>
> Afford all interested persons reasonable opportunity to submit data, views, or arguments in writing. Opportunity for public hearing may be granted if requested in a timely manner and determined by the sponsoring department to be

in the public interest. It is the intent of this Act that reasonable and timely requests for public hearings be favorably acted upon by the sponsoring department. Following the close of the public comment period, and prior to making its final recommendation to the Tribal Council, the department shall fully consider all oral comments and written submissions respecting the proposed action.[52]

Public participation is recognized and accommodated by many tribes, as demonstrated under the Puyallup APA, and other similarly enacted tribal administrative procedure acts. The key procedures provide for notice of the rulemaking, an opportunity for community members to participate by submitting comments, views, or arguments in writing or at a public hearing, and to have their oral or written comments considered by the tribal agency. These tribal procedures for public participation are similar to the federal APA. Adherence to good rulemaking is important for tribes and affected industry. Such procedures will likely result in a more carefully considered rule, but also may increase confidence of the regulated community by assuring more opportunity for formal participation in the development of the rules and regulations by which they will be governed.

The use of regulatory boards of experts to adopt regulations and overhear disputes is well established at the state and federal level. Tribes might well profit from the adoption of such a framework, and from the board members possessing a wide range of expertise and perspective. Inclusion of non-tribal representatives on tribal boards, and perhaps including representatives from the regulated community may prove to be useful. Industry representatives have significant expertise to lend to such boards. Also, different perspectives help governing bodies make informed decisions. A tribe that is secure in its authority to regulate environmental matters need not confirm that authority by staffing its regulatory boards exclusively with tribal members; significant gain in expertise and perspective may result from a more diverse composition of the regulatory board.

For example, in 1995, the Shoshone-Bannock Tribes and the FMC Corporation in Idaho entered into an agreement on the regulatory authority of the Tribes over the industry, including permitting, regulations, and fees. As part of this agreement, the parties agreed to an administrative committee to facilitate and implement the agreement for rulemaking, non-attainment matters, permitting, as well as to address other matters. The seven-member committee was comprised of two tribal representatives, two from FMC, one EPA representative, one State of Idaho representative, and one at-large member selected by the other six representatives. Any disputes under the agreement were handled by a special panel of the Tribal Court consisting of three attorney members–one selected by the Tribes, one selected by FMC and one selected by the two panel members.

2. Due Process in Adjudication

Adjudication occurs when an agency or department of the tribe makes a decision, such as acting on a permit application, enforcement action, a contested action or violation by a permittee, or issuance of a major decision affecting the rights of individuals or companies. Simply stated, if an agency makes a decision that affects an individual on grounds that are particularized to the individual, then the agency has engaged in adjudication.

When an adjudication occurs, the fundamental requirements of due process apply and provide that a person whose property interests may be adversely affected by a proposed governmental action be given notice, an opportunity to be heard, a fair hearing, and a decision based upon the relevant facts and applicable legal standards. The precise procedural safeguards applicable to a given case depend on consideration of the following factors:

> First, the private interest that will be affected by the official action; second, the risk of erroneous deprivation of such interest through the procedures used, and probable value, if any, of additional or substitute procedural safeguards; and finally, the government's interest, including function involved and the fiscal and administrative burdens that the additional or substitute procedural requirements would entail.[53]

As discussed in Chapter 2, tribal constitutions and other laws may establish due process and equal protection procedures as matters of tribal law. Also, the Indian Civil Rights Act incorporates due process, equal protection and other limitations on the exercise of governmental power as such limitations apply to tribal administrative agencies. Tribal APAs supplement the minimum requirements of the due process by establishing criteria for tribal agency decision-making, establishing rules and evidentiary requirements for contested cases, and setting procedures and standards for administrative appeals and judicial review of administrative actions. These administrative procedures provide greater certainty and predictability and greater openness and accountability than is required by the due process clause itself.

Tribal administrative laws establish procedural requirements for administrative appeals and judicial review of administrative actions. For instance, the requirements for timeliness of a notice of appeal to a commission or petition for judicial review are covered in tribal APAs. Tribal laws also set notice requirements for contested cases (i.e. statement of time, place, and notice of hearing, statement of authority and jurisdiction of authority, and issue and matters to be decided).[54] Many tribal administrative laws establish substantive standards for administrative appeals, such as the appeal to be made on the record developed before the administrative appeals board or commission.[55] This means that the briefs, pleadings, evidence, decisions and orders received and issued by a tribal commission or board will be considered by the reviewing tribal court upon appeal.

For instance, in Montana, the Confederated Salish and Kootenai Tribal Administrative Procedure Ordinance provides that:

If a timely petition for review of a commission decision is filed for judicial review, the tribal administrative laws provide that the court may affirm the final decision of the agency or uphold the promulgation of the rule, it may remand the case for further proceedings, or it may reverse the final decision or the rule, in whole or part, if the substantial rights of the petitioners have been prejudiced because the administrative findings, inferences, conclusions, or decisions are in violation of constitutional provisions, in excess of lawful authority or jurisdiction, clearly erroneous or arbitrary or capricious.[56]

Such provisions are very similar to the federal and state APAs.

Tribal administrative procedures acts/ordinances provide a guide for tribal environmental programs to address issues associated with implementation of the tribal laws and the regulation of activities affecting natural resources in tribal communities. The tribal administrative procedure acts seek to ensure that their administrative bodies carry out their programs consistent with the notions of common sense, justice and fairness. They institutionalize public participation by establishing a process that:

(1) Requires public participation through oral and written comment;
(2) Promotes honesty and integrity in the process;
(3) Offers a means for public hearings;
(4) Fosters predictability and greater certainty to the community; and
(5) Ensures that the comments, questions and concerns of the community will be recorded and considered by the tribal agencies.

The Tribal administrative procedures laws provide for limited waivers of tribal sovereign immunity. Typically, the relief provided under the laws, do not include monetary judgments against the tribal sovereign. In Washington, under the Puyallup Tribes and Confederated Colville Tribes APAs the Tribal Courts can affirm or remand the Tribal administrative agency's actions on a permit, license or administrative order, but the Tribal Court is not authorized to enter a monetary judgment against the Tribe.[57]

Additionally, tribal APAs create supplemental due process requirements to those found in the tribal constitution, tribal civil rights acts and/or ICRA. The APAs ensure that when a tribal action or proposed action may affect an individual's property:

That individual is to be given notice, an opportunity to be heard by the administrative body, receive a fair hearing and a decision upon the relevant facts, and be able to seek judicial review of the administrative decision.

These basic requirements certainly meet the fundamental requirements of due process. A tribal APA can be a mechanism for achieving goals of certainty, fairness, timeliness, and technical expertise. The simple existence of the mechanism can provide the regulated industry with some degree of confidence, and tribes with greater credibility as industry is accustomed to operating by established administrative procedures in other jurisdictions. An APA is not the only means of constructing a framework for environmental regulation; specific environmental laws and regulations may describe the administrative process for certain specific regulations.

B.   Other Measures to Ensure Meaningful Public Participation

In 2000, the Indigenous Peoples Subcommittee published a "Guide on Consultation and Collaboration with Indian Tribal Governments and the Public Participation of Indigenous Groups and Tribal Members in Environmental Decision Making." The Guide, an impetus for this document, includes a plan setting forth certain guiding principles and critical elements tribal governments should consider for effective public participation.[58] Two key guiding principles are:

(1) Encourage public participation by having interactions that encourage active community participation, institutionalize public participation, recognize knowledge and utilize cross-cultural formats and exchanges; and

(2) Maintain honesty and integrity by establishing the goals, expectations and limitations early in the process.

The critical elements include a means for meeting preparation, meeting participation, logistics, agenda setting, information-sharing, and seeking and gaining valuable community input. These are good starting points, but more is needed in terms of practical approaches and processes for tribal governments.

Certainly, the approaches to accomplishing these critical elements will vary according to the tribal community and culture, tribal commitment, the particular issue and decision, and resources the tribal government may have to seek public participation. Tribes have an opportunity to develop innovative measures outside of the administrative law context to effectively provide meaningful public participation for their communities. Continuing education of the community, two-way communication, responsiveness, and information sharing are vital components to effectively gain community support and input.

Establishing a community advisory board or committee for the environmental program, as discussed earlier, may prove helpful in gaining a community and cultural perspective that may be different than the governmental decision-making body. An advisory board used in the initial stages of a rulemaking can help:

Generate questions, identify public concerns, make recommendations, provide independent views on issues, formulate meeting formats, and give insight on locations for meetings, stakeholders or segments of the community whose comments should be sought out.

The advisory board could meet on a monthly or quarterly basis depending on the environmental program activities. In addition, a community working group comprised of a variety of tribal, non-tribal and industry representatives may assist in draft rulemaking and review, prior to public comments being solicited.

Some tribes have explored the issue of providing non-members with meaningful opportunities to be involved and treated fairly by developing innovative approaches from a tribal perspective. This is a timely issue as tribal environmental laws are increasingly regulating non-member activities and industry continues to bring economic development to reservations. The Tulalip Tribes of Washington, for example, has enacted a Planning Enabling Act[59] that provides non-members a fair voice in tribal land use planning. Like many checker-boarded reservations, the Tulalip Reservation is held in both trust and fee simple ownership after the sale of Indian allotments made during the early 20th Century. Reflecting the Tribes' desire for good governance in tribal land use decision-making, the Act requires that:

> "At least two members of the Tulalip Planning Commission be
> non-Indian persons residing, occupying or owning land located
> within the exterior boundaries of the Tulalip Indian Reservation."

These types of advisory boards of tribal members and/or non-tribal members can prove helpful in establishing trust in a community and bringing together a cross-section of the tribal community.

Oftentimes, going out to the community to seek tribal member input rather than requesting them to come to the government office is productive. Holding small group meetings at tribal district or chapter halls will gain more public participation than at a large community hearing. Tribal members are more likely to ask questions and give their opinion in a smaller community setting. Tribal environmental programs may schedule open houses to encourage tribal members to attend without the pressure of being recorded or feeling as though they have to offer a comment. This atmosphere allows individuals to review the project and talk one-on-one with the program staff. A short survey wherein the responder can remain anonymous can also prove valuable if information or comments are sought on a specific issue. Of course, the survey has to be carefully drafted to clearly and concisely gain a response without any built in biases, and the staff must be willing to undertake interviews using the survey instrument. It may also prove helpful to involve representatives from various stakeholders in developing the survey, if one is to be used.

In 1999, the Gila River Indian Community in Arizona established an Environmental Quality Compliance and Enforcement Policy, which includes an outreach program to assist the regulated facilities in voluntarily complying with the Tribe's environmental laws.[60] This Policy advocates education and technical assistance, and requires the Department of Environmental Quality to:

> "(1) Provide technical assistance to regulated community, as resources permit; (2) provide current rules, policies and guidelines to affected and interested parties; and (3) provide compliance education opportunities for the regulated community."[61]

This Policy encourages the environmental programs to seek public participation, to inform through education and information dissemination, and draft clear and consistent rules and regulations. Although the Gila River Tribal Policy does not specifically state "public participation," "meaningful involvement" or "fair treatment," the Policy addresses and implements these fundamental principles.

All of these measures require a commitment on the part of the tribal environmental programs to be more proactive and to solicit input from the community rather than meeting the bare minimum standards of public participation. These measures are intended to foster public awareness and make the government decision-making processes more open to the public. It is through these measures that tribal governments can begin to gain input from its tribal community and build support for its decision-making.

C.   Tribal Examples Effectively Providing Meaningful Public Participation and Fair Treatment

In addition to some tribes adopting administrative procedures laws, policies and guidelines and advisory boards to ensure fair treatment and meaningful public participation, there are tribes who have developed other fair treatment and meaningful involvement measures for reservation residents. Some specific examples are presented below: (1) the Alaska Native villages process of meaningful involvement; (2) Confederated Tribes of the Colville Reservation Holistic Approach to Resources Management; and (3) Shoshone-Bannock Tribes Minority Communications Board.

The work of the Maniilaq Association in Kotzebue (northwest Alaska)[62] highlights the continuing importance and use of oral traditions in Alaska Native villages. Many of the Alaska Native villages are still very rural and isolated with no road system into or out of the villages while access is generally by airplane or boat. In these communities, interaction and communication is by word of mouth. Direct, one-to-one communication with the local official and decision-maker on environmental issues is the standard, and the best means of providing input. Certainly, this process is ideal for small communities where everyone knows one another, families go back many generations, and there is established trust and goodwill. Traditional observations and knowledge are also important and play a central role in decision-making.

The public process of gathering comments and input on land management and environmental issues often begins with the posting of notices at the community post office and stores, announcements on the public radio stations, communication via citizen band radios, and direct contact with individuals. A meeting is held and comments gathered. There are no set limits on oral presentations by members, no guidelines or restrictions on the length of the meeting although the meetings generally are long since many individuals express their opinions. Again, this follows the Native traditions. The process is generally informal which is conducive to good communication. The language spoken is the native language. Often, the decision-makers gather comments or input by tape recordings in small groups or gatherings, take trips to the homes to communicate with elders and family leaders, or talk with individuals as they visit with them in the community. Written comments are rarely received. In addition to the posted meetings, the environmental managers distribute monthly and quarterly newsletters to all residents of the community to give updates and solicit participation. Daily interactions between the environmental staff and community members are a priority. There is no established written protocol or process for these public meetings, but they are successful in addressing the needs and concerns of the community. This process based upon Alaska Native traditions provides for meaningful involvement of community members.

Secondly, the Confederated Tribes of the Colville Reservation in Washington created a holistic resource management approach to gather community input from their tribal membership on a resource management plan including environmental regulation. Importantly, the Colville Tribe recognized that:

> Its community members had the right to participate fully in formulating, planning, managing and applying governmental regulations, and environmental decisions affecting tribal and individually held lands and resources.

The project was an ambitious one that was completed over a two year period, and it is a model for identifying issues and matters affecting the health, culture and environment of the people, organizing community support, acquiring tribal member input and establishing creative methods of gathering and responding to tribal member needs and rights. The project gathered information and input at tribal district meetings, community gatherings, special meetings, one-on-one interviews, and public meetings. The Tribe provided written presentations, handouts and clearly documented goals and objectives for Tribal members to comment on. The Tribal program staff ensured that they were responsive to Tribal members' needs and inquiries to facilitate and empower the Tribal community. The results of the project have enabled the Tribe to formulate Tribal goals, future visions, and resources management plans for the Reservation, which holds a variety of resources managed by the Tribe.

The third illustration is the establishment of a "Minority Communications Board" by the Shoshone-Bannock Tribes in Idaho.[63] The Board was established in 1979 for the following reasons:

> "The Tribes have existed as a minority for more than a century, and thus are highly aware of the feelings of frustration and helplessness associated with minority status. To ensure a voice on land use matters for non-Indians who reside on the Reservation and

who are ineligible to vote in Tribal elections by virtue of the Tribal Constitution and Bylaws, the [Land Use Policy] Commission shall appoint a board to be known as the "Minority Communication Board."[64]

The purpose of the three-member Board is to "provide a vehicle for communication and cooperation between the Tribes and non-Indians residing on the Reservation."

> The Land Use Policy Commission works "with the Board to ensure that the land use problems and needs of non-Indians are expressed, and that the legitimate land use rights of non-Indians are protected."[65]

The Board meets on a quarterly basis with the Commission to discuss issues, gather information about the status of various environmental matters, give input on pending matters, raise questions and voice concerns that they may have about tribal land use issues and environmental programs. The Board has proved useful in building non-Indian support for Tribal jurisdiction over non-Indians on a wide variety of issues beyond environmental regulation. The Board distributes information to other non-Indian landowners about the Tribal programs, permits, and other regulations that are required throughout the Reservation. Non-Indians routinely telephone or contact the Tribal Land Use and environmental programs about possible violators of Tribal law, for assistance with potential pollution discharges, to inquiry about permits and a myriad of other issues.

The Fort Hall Reservation is comprised of 97% tribal trust lands and 3% fee lands owned by individual tribal members and non-Indians. The Tribes instituted this process over 35 years ago, and it has proved successful in gathering input and providing for public participation of all residents of the reservation. The Confederated Salish and Kootenai Tribes of the Flathead Reservation in Montana have established a similar board to provide for meaningful involvement of reservation residents. The Flathead Reservation is severely checkerboarded with non-Indians owning a majority of the reservation lands. The Tribes initiated this board after non-Indians challenged their jurisdiction during the approval of their treatment as a state application under the Clean Water Act.

D. EPA's Role In Meeting the Charge

Beginning in 1970, with the National Environmental Policy Act (NEPA), the United States Congress officially "recognized the profound impact of man's activities on the interrelationship of all components of the natural environment . . . [and] the critical importance of restoring and maintaining environmental quality to the overall welfare and development of man . . ."[66] To this end, the federal government has committed billions of dollars in funding and technical resources to the states for building environmental institutions, drafting codes and regulations, and compliance and enforcement to administer the various environmental protection programs contemplated in federal environmental legislation. The NEJAC emphasizes that recognition of equitable tribal capacity building to protect tribal lands and resources is needed.

Tribal governments share the same environmental concerns as the states, and therefore need similar support.

Congress adopted NEPA and other federal environmental laws aimed at preserving and reclaiming environmental integrity, but did not, originally, fully integrate American Indian and Alaska Natives or effectively address the role tribal governments would play in regulating activities affecting the environment on tribal lands. EPA's authority to delegate responsibilities for the implementation and management of the various federal environmental programs to the states was expressly included in the original statutes as adopted. Tribes have been working hard to obtain favorable interpretation of the federal environmental laws, and are successfully working with Congress and the EPA to amend the federal laws to include tribes. Providing tribes with effective tribal regulatory powers to maintain management of tribal lands needs to be a priority.

Today, many federal statutes permit EPA to authorize tribes to run the federal environmental programs. EPA has been a leader in its commitment to assist in the legislative amendments and to provide assistance to tribes. However, additional technical support and funding are needed to help develop their environmental programs. EPA and Congress specifically, have committed over 30 years and billions of dollars to building state environmental programs, environmental management and enforcement infrastructures.[67] Regulatory development funding and technical assistance from the federal government needs to be increased to help tribes develop and implement more effective environmental programs. EPA has an unparalleled opportunity to help tribes attain environmental integrity within their reservations.

There are great differences among tribes in their capabilities and desire to actually exercise their sovereign powers in the area of environmental management. Some have well-developed and sophisticated governmental institutions which function effectively. Other tribal governments are in great need of technical assistance, training programs, and stable sources of funding in order to function to their full potential and serve the needs of their people. Some tribal environmental programs are ineffective, in part, due to the lack or inadequacy of financial resources and institutional development.

Tribal environmental programs are evolving at a rapid rate and are in the early stages of developing ordinances and regulations for the tribal community. Some tribes may not have a process to provide for meaningful public participation and fair treatment within their established infrastructure. Certainly, tribal agencies can learn from other tribal examples and federal processes and consider how such processes can be incorporated by the tribe, taking into account their particular tribal values, and cultural and social norms. Some tribes do not have the staff or expertise to develop these procedures and processes. Training could be offered at national or regional EPA meetings, or be provided upon request by a specific tribe. Furthermore, training could be developed by various tribal organizations.

Many tribes need financial and technical support to fully develop and implement their ordinances and processes. Additional regulations, administrative procedures, or other mechanisms to ensure public participation and fair treatment increase the burden on new programs and utilize the limited resources available for program implementation. A new program that is inadequately funded or staffed is likely to fail, wasting the limited resources that exist. Effective and efficient programs require funds, training and technical expertise.

NEJAC' Advice and Recommendations

Advice

3.1   EPA should recognize that tribal perspectives relating to individual rights and tribal communal rights vary, and that these perspectives have implications for meaningful involvement and fair treatment in Indian country and in Alaska Native villages.

3.2   EPA should recognize the current economic conditions facing tribes, and how these conditions impact tribal government efforts to provide basic governmental services, including environmental and public health protection, and the development and implementation of meaningful involvement and fair treatment processes.

3.3   EPA should recognize the impacts of colonialism upon traditional tribal governments, and how these impacts affect tribal governments' efforts to implement federal environmental laws, including requirements for public participation and due process. (See Appendix B)

3.4   EPA should recognize the impacts of the federal allotment policy on tribal jurisdiction and initiate training to help sensitize and educate persons living or working within the exterior boundaries of the reservation. (See Appendix B)

Recommendations

3.5   In fulfilling part of its trust responsibility, EPA should consult with tribes on how the information, advice and recommendations provided in this document can be best used by tribes to provide for, or enhance, meaningful involvement and fair treatment when tribes develop and implement federally-approved tribal environmental programs.

3.6   EPA should develop materials to inform tribal governments about the federal environmental laws and regulations requiring public participation and due process.

3.7   EPA should work with tribal members and community-based organizations to understand their perspectives and interests in public involvement and due process methods for federally-approved tribal environmental programs.

3.8   EPA should support and give deference to tribal institutional definitions of due process and public participation, which will tend to be based on tribal culture, traditions, government structure, and social norms.

3.9   EPA should work collaboratively with tribes to develop training and education for tribes, tribal members, and tribal community-based organizations on meaningful involvement and fair treatment.

3.10   EPA should assist the tribes who are interested in developing administrative procedures (including processes for public participation and due process) so they will be better prepared to develop and implement federally-approved tribal environmental programs.

3.11   EPA should work collaboratively with tribes to ensure that federally-approved tribal environmental programs provide for effective public participation and due process.

3.12   EPA should support coordination and collaboration among the tribes that have established meaningful involvement and fair treatment processes with the tribes seeking to develop their own processes.

3.13   EPA should help the tribes interested in fostering a dialogue with business and industry, states, local governments, and non-members on the issues of sovereignty, jurisdiction, and land ownership, which are likely to arise in the development and implementation of meaningful involvement and fair treatment processes.

3.14   EPA should recognize the unique situation of Alaska Natives with respect to the implementation of federal environmental laws in Alaska, and develop a better understanding of how to work with Alaska Native Tribes to address the multiplicity of environmental issues they face, including meaningful involvement and fair treatment in the development and implementation of federal environmental laws by EPA and the State of Alaska, and the State's environmental laws.

3.15   EPA needs to ensure there are adequate resources (technical and financial), and offer, financial and technical assistance to tribes to promote and provide for meaningful involvement and fair treatment in federally-approved tribal environmental programs. Funding should be set-aside specifically for these purposes.

CONCLUSION

The basic tribal traditional values of fairness, respect, honesty, the opportunity to speak before a collective decision is made, consensus decision-making, and careful and thoughtful deliberation predate any constitutional provisions or civil rights laws. These universal tribal understandings of fairness are handed down by word of mouth, without any written mandate or instruction. This document has explored how to best accommodate, define and incorporate these fundamental tribal teachings of due process and meaningful involvement within the tribal context as they relate to environmental regulatory authority.

This document has offered a candid discussion of the tensions between the adoption of European-style government principles of due process and reliance upon tribal customs and traditions; urged tribal governments to provide for meaningful involvement and fair treatment of the tribal community at-large; and stressed the challenges tribes will likely face if they do not provide opportunities for public participation and due process. This document has offered numerous tribal examples and models, standards, tribal laws, administrative procedures and policies addressing fair treatment and public participation that are working effectively in Indian country and in Alaska. The NEJAC anticipates that these recommendations may, in some measure, add to the development of tribal environmental programs as they serve their people and community, and protect and preserve the integrity of tribal culture and homelands.

ENDNOTES

1 Credit should be given to Dean Suagee, a former IPS Subcommittee member, for his innovative thoughts and ideas in this area. His opinion and advocacy on the issues of public participation and due process for tribal regulatory programs led the IPS Subcommittee to consider the issues when it wrote its first document on Consultation with Tribal Governments, and assisted the past Subcommittee in the initial outline of this document. Mr. Suagee has informed the IPS that he wrote an article on the issues addressed in this document. See Dean Suagee, Due Process and Public Participation In Tribal Environmental Programs, 13 Tul. Envtl. L.J. 1 (1999). Although the NEJAC did not know of or rely upon his article in drafting this document, we wish to recognize his work in the area.

2 The IPS has struggled with the use of the phrase "fair treatment" given the history of abuse and federal policies developed toward Indian people and nations. Dean Suagee also discusses the difficulties in applying the EPA's Environmental Justice principles and policies to tribal governments and people in his paper, "Dimensions of Environmental Justice in Indian Country and Native Alaska," Second National People of Color Environmental Leadership Summit – Summit II, October 23, 2002, Environmental Justice Resource center at Clark Atlanta University.

3 U.S Environmental Protection Agency, Environmental Justice Homepage: www.epa.gov/compliance.environmentaljustice; see also Exec. Order No. 12898, 59 Fed. Reg. 7629 (Feb. 11, 1994).

4 Id.

5 Oglala Sioux Court, Civ. Ap. 90-348 at 5-6 (1991) (holding that due process requires a hearing before attempting to remove anyone from the Pine Ridge Reservation).

6 *Begay v. Navajo Nation*, 15 Indian L. Rptr. 6032, 6034 (Navajo Sp. Ct. 1988).

7 Constitution of Spokane Tribe – Spokane Reservation, Wellpinit, Washington, Const. Art. IV, § 1.

8 Rosebud Sioux Tribe Constitution, Art. V, Section 3, Bill of Rights. See also, Art. VII, Bill of Rights, Constitution and Bylaws of the Makah Indian Tribal of the Makah Indian Reservation, Washington; Art. VII, Bill of Rights, Constitution and Bylaws for the Tulalip Tribe of Washington.

9 Chapter 1-5, Adopted 02/04/88, Certified 02/16/88, Res. 1988-76.

10 E.g., Puyallup Tribal Administrative Procedure Act, Section 1.4 (1993). See also Colville Administrative Procedure Act, and Salish and Kootnai Administrative Procedure Ordinance.

11 See generally Christine Zuni, Strengthening What Remains, 7 KAN.L.J. & PUB. POL'Y 17 (1997).

12 25 U.S.C. §§1301 – 1303 (1994). The ICRA was enacted over the objections of many tribal governments, some of which believed that economic burdens of compliance would be too great and others, especially the Pueblos of New Mexico, which felt their own cultural traditions were superior to "white man's justice." Witnesses also testified that tribal traditions of fairness and justice made the ICRA an unnecessary intrusion on tribal sovereignty.

13 The Indian Civil Rights Act: A Report of the United States Commission on Civil Rights 5 (June 1991).

14 Constitution of Jamestown S'Klallam Tribe of Indians, Art. IX, Bill of Rights.

[15] Constitution of the Skokomish Indian Tribe (May 3, 1938), as amended March 17, 1980, Article IV – Rights of Individuals.

[16] 436 U.S. 49 (1978). At issue in *Santa Clara* was a tribal ordinance enacted by the Santa Clara Pueblo in 1939 barring from tribal membership children of female tribal members married to non-members. The Supreme Court ruled that the ICRA only provided relief by writ of habeas corpus and did not waive tribal sovereign immunity.

[17] See, e.g. *In re The Sacred Arrows,* 3 Okla. Trib. 332, 337-38 (D. Ct. Cheyenne-Arapaho Tribes 1990) ("Anglo-American concepts of fairness and civil rights are sometimes inappropriate, in their raw form, to Indian communities. These concepts can be applied only in conjunction with the unique cultural, social and political attributes of Indian heritage.").

[18] See *Colville Confederated Tribes v. St. Peter,* 20 Indian L. Rep. 6108, 6110 (Colv. Ct. App. 1993) ("We . . . apply due process principles under ICRA with flexibility and in a manner contextually adapted by the Colville Confederated Tribes.").

[19] *Berry v. Arapahoe and Shoshone Tribes,* 420 F. Supp. 934, 943-44 (D. Wyo. 1976).

[20] *Stands Over Bull v. Bureau of Indian Affairs,* 442 F. Supp. 360, 376 (D. Mont. 1977).

[21] *Johnson v. Lower Elwha Tribal Community,* 484 F.2d 200, 203 (9th Cir. 1973).

[22] *Poodry v. Tonawanda Band of Seneca Indians,* 85 F.3d 874 (2d. Cir. 1996).

[23] International Covenant on Civil and Political Rights, G.A. Res. 2000A (XXI) 21UNGAOR Supp. (No. 16) at 52, U.S. Doc. A/6316 (1996), 999 U.N.T.S. 171 entered into force March 23, 1976.

[24] G.A. Res. 217(A) III, Dec. 10, 1948, U.N. Doc. A/810, at 71.

[25] See Draft Declaration on the Rights of Indigenous Peoples, E/CN.4/Sub.2/1994/2/Add.1 (1994). The Draft Declaration, which is the leading international document on the rights of indigenous peoples, was drafted over an eight-year period by the Working Group on Indigenous Peoples, and submitted to the United Nations Commission on Human Rights' Sub-Commission on the Prevention of Discrimination and Protection of Minorities. The Sub-Commission approved the document in 1994.

[26] OAS, GR/DADIN/doc.23/01 (11May 2001).

[27] Id. at Article II.

[28] Id. at Article XIII, 1, 2, 4.

[29] Id. at Article XVIII, 4.

[30] Id. at 5.

[31] The American Indian Religious Freedom Act of 1978, S.J. Res. 102, Aug. 11, 1978, Pub. L. No. 95-341, codified in part 42 U.S.C. § 1996.

[32] 25 U.SC. §§ 3001-13.

[33] 40 C.F.R. § 25.1 (1999).

[34] 40 C.F.R. § 131.20(b).

[35] 40 C.F.R. § 25.4.

[36] See 40 C.F.R. §§ 124.1 and 124.1(e) (1999).

[37] 40 C.F.R. §§ 124.6(e), (b)-(c), 124.10(a)-(b), 124.11, 124.19.

[38] 42 U.S.C. § 4321 (1994).

[39] 42 U.S.C. § 4332 (2) (C). These statutory requirements are implemented under regulations issued by the President's Council on Environmental Quality (CEQ). 40 C.F.R. Parts. 1500-08 (1996).

[40] The Tulalip Tribes in Washington and the Rosebud Sioux Tribe of South Dakota have established such environmental review processes.

[41] 40 C.F.R. § 1508.8.5. In 1999, the CEQ issued a guidance urging federal agencies to more actively involve tribes as cooperating agencies. CEQ. Memorandum for Head of Federal Agencies, 1999.

[42] "Public Involvement Policy of the U.S. Environmental Protection Agency, May 2003, U.S. Environmental Protection Agency, Document #EPA233-B-03-002.

[43] Id. at 1.

[44] Id. at 1-2.

[45] Id. at 5-6.

[46] Id. at 7, Appendix 1 –Guidance for Implementing Public Involvement at EPA.

[47] In 1996, Michael O'Connell wrote a comprehensive paper on administrative law and its application to tribal governments. The paper and its tribal administrative body examples have been relied upon and utilized in this section of the report. See "Tribal Administrative Law" presented at the American Bar Association 8th Annual Conference on Environment and Development in Indian Country, November 7-8, 1996, Albuquerque, New Mexico.

[48] *Id.*

[49] B. Schwartz. Administrative Law at 1. (3d Ed. 1991).

[50] 5 U.S.C. §§ 551-559 (1994 & Supp. 1998).

[51] See supra note 10, Puyallup Tribal, and Colville Tribal Administrative Acts, and Salish and Kootenai Administrative Procedure Ordinance. See also Three Affiliated Tribes Administrative Procedure Act.

[52] Puyallup Tribal Administrative Procedure Act, Section 1.4.

[53] *Matthews v. Eldridge*, 424 U.S. 319, 335 (1976).

[54] Puyallup Tribal Administrative Procedure Act, Section 1.12, supra note 10.

[55] Colville Administrative Procedure Act, Section 2-4-19(7); Puyallup Administrative Procedure Act, Section 1.19(7).

[56] Salish & Kootenai Tribal Administrative Procedure Ordinance, Section 28(a), Section 29(4), supra note 10; Three Affiliated Tribes Administrative Procedure Act, Section 1.12(4) and 1.15, supra note 10.

[57] Puyallup APA, Section 1.97(7); Colville APA, Section 2-4-19(7).

[58] Addendum D in "Guide on Consultation and Collaboration with Indian Tribal Governments and Public Participation of Indigenous Groups and Tribal Members in Environmental Decision Making," November 2000, U.S. Environmental Protection Agency, Document # 300-R-00-009.

[59] Section 4 Tulalip Tribes Planning Enabling Act.

[60] Gila River Indian Community "Department of Environmental Interim Compliance and Enforcement Policy," Initial Date: February 5, 1999. Revised June 1, 2001.

[61] Id. at 1.

[62] Hazel Apok, Environmental Program Director, Maniilaq Association, provided the information on the Alaska Native oral traditions to the IPS.

[63] Shoshone-Bannock Tribes "Fort Hall Land Use Operative Policy Guidelines," September 27, 1979, Chapter VI.

[64] Id. at Section VI-1.

[65] Id. at Section VI-2.

[66] 42 U.S.C. 4331(a).

[67] See Judith V. Royster and Rory Snowarrow Fausett, "Control of the Reservation Environment: Tribal Primacy, Federal Delegation, and the Limits of State Intrusion," 54 WASH. L.REV. 581, 629-630 (1989).

NEJAC/Indigenous Peoples Subcommittee
Tribal Environmental Justice

Charge

Addressing the environmental justice issues facing Native Americans requires an understanding of the complexities of federal Indian law and policies. Environmental justice issues facing Native Americans are quite varied. One of the primary issues pertains to the inadequate technical and financial support for tribal government environmental and public health protection programs, such as: 1) solid waste management, 2) surface water, groundwater and drinking water protection, 3) management and disposal of toxic substances, 4) air quality management, and 5) lack of consistent and effective federal direct implementation of environmental programs in Indian country. Other issues pertain to the impacts on tribal treaty rights, usual and accustomed use areas, cultural resources, and sacred places, both on or off the reservations. A further set of issues pertain to the lack of <u>meaningful involvement</u> and <u>fair treatment</u> of tribal members and others when federal environmental programs are managed or implemented in Indian country or in areas of interest to Alaska Natives.

In 2000, the National Environmental Justice Advisory Council (NEJAC) produced a document, "Guide on Consultation and Collaboration with Indian Tribal Governments and the Public Participation of Indigenous Groups and Tribal Members in Environmental Decision Making," which did an outstanding job of discussing how federal agencies, like EPA, can most effectively work with tribes. The document also touched on the importance of providing for meaningful public participation and fair treatment, which are fundamental principles of environmental justice. However, the Guide does not go into detail about how meaningful public participation or fair treatment could be pursued by tribal governments.

The Agency recognizes it has a responsibility to work with tribal governments, as it does with state and local governments, to support their efforts to address environmental justice issues, especially those which pertain to the implementation of federal environmental law. The Agency, therefore, is asking the Indigenous Peoples Subcommittee, through the NEJAC, to provide advice and recommendations on the following question:

How should EPA work with tribes to identify and address environmental justice issues arising within Indian country and of concern to Alaska Natives related to the development and implementation of federally authorized/approved tribal environmental programs?

(a)   In what ways should EPA assist Tribal governments to provide <u>meaningful public involvement</u> in the development and implementation of federally authorized and/or approved tribal environmental programs? Attention should be given to the following areas:

(1)   involvement of tribal members and tribal community organizations
(2)   involvement of non-tribal residents
(3)   involvement of other stakeholders (on or off the reservation)

(b)   In what ways should EPA assist Tribal governments to provide <u>fair treatment</u> of all stakeholders in the development and implementation of federally authorized and/or approved tribal environmental programs? Attention should be given to the following areas:

(1)   treatment of tribal members and tribal community organizations
(2)   treatment of non-tribal residents
(3)   treatment of other stakeholders (on or off the reservation)

In sum, what short-term and long-term actions should the Agency take to assist tribes to address the meaningful involvement and fair treatment issues in Indian country and of concern to Alaska Natives related to the development and implementation of federally authorized/approved tribal environmental programs.

Significant Federal Policies Impacting Tribes

I.   Background

The IPS believes that EPA should have a fundamental understanding of the history of relations between American Indian and Alaska Native tribes and the federal government, the unique political status of tribes in the United States, and the special trust relationship that EPA and other federal agencies have with tribes. These federal policies and trust obligation are discussed in this appendix. Additionally, in Section C, this appendix presents the regulatory jurisdiction of tribes over environmental matters occurring on reservations. It is only through this understanding that the EPA, and readers of this document, will be able to grasp the complex issues and concepts discussed, comprehend the advice and recommendations offered by the IPS, as well as appreciate the opportunities and challenges the EPA will face in working with tribes to provide for meaningful involvement and fair treatment in the development and implementation of federally authorized/approved tribal environmental programs.

This appendix presents four distinct periods of federal Indian policy (although there are others) primarily applicable to the lower 48 tribes. These four periods, commonly known as allotment, reorganization, termination, and self-determination, have impacted tribal sovereignty and are relevant to this document. Over a 130-year period, the overriding purposes of the federal government changed dramatically, shifting back and forth between two fundamentally different visions of the future of Indian people in American society. During the allotment and termination eras, the overriding premise was that Indians, as individuals, should be assimilated into mainstream American society, and that Indian nations as politically distinct governments, should cease to exist. In contrast, during the reorganization and self-determination eras, federal policy supported the continued existence of tribes as politically distinct communities. These ever-changing federal policies significantly impacted tribal governments.

Although some of these federal policies impacted Alaska Natives, the situation for Alaska Native tribes is fundamentally different then tribes in the lower 48 due to the Alaska Native Claims Settlement Act[1]. The IPS sees the need to provide a separate discussion of Alaska Native land and resources, and governmental and corporate structure issues in this appendix. The IPS calls upon the EPA to recognize the unique situation of Alaska Natives with respect to EPA tribal environmental initiatives, and to consider ways to best address the numerous pollution controls and environmental injustices on Alaska Native lands. The IPS also recommends that the EPA consider conducting a separate study to review and address the myriad of environmental issues facing Alaska Natives, and the unique legal status of Alaska Natives.

A. Allotment

Prior to 1871, when treaty-making with tribes ended, Congress recognized tribal governments through treaties, and tribes retained sovereignty over their territories. From 1871 to

---

[1]   85 Stat. 688, 43 U.S.C.

1934, federal policy changed to one of assimilation, further diminishing tribal self-government. For many, the allotment era, beginning in 1871, was the most devastating historical blow to tribalism and Indian life, impacting tribal cultures on a massive scale. This period of federal Indian policy converted some tribally-held communal lands to individual land ownership. This was the principle legal mechanism by which the assimilation policy was carried out. During this era, the federal government attacked the core value of tribal cultures on several fronts: traditional religious practices were outlawed; children were taken away to off-reservation boarding schools; tribal landholdings were confiscated and converted into individual allotments: the so called "surplus" lands were made available for settlement by non-Indians; and traditional tribal institutions were undermined and weakened.[2]

The linchpin of this policy was the Dawes Act, also known as the General Allotment Act of 1887.[3] President Theodore Roosevelt most forcefully described this Act as "a mighty pulverizing engine to break up the tribal mass. It acts directly upon the family and the individual."[4] The results of the allotment period are truly devastating, including a loss of about two thirds of Indian lands: tribal lands were reduced from 138 million in 1887 to 52 million by 1934.[5] More than 26 million acres of allotted land were transferred from the tribe to individual Indian allottees and then to non-Indians through purchase, fraud, mortgage, foreclosures and tax sales, which has resulted in the contemporary presence of a substantial number of non-Indians living within the boundaries of many Indian reservations.[6] For the first time, reservations became checkerboarded, consisting of tribal, individual Indian, individual non-Indian, and corporate properties.

When the reservations were opened to settlement, traditional governments were severely impacted and the authority of the tribes was undermined by the Bureau of Indian Affairs (BIA) agents. The great influx of non-Indian settlers, coupled with the loss of communal lands and the federal government's policies outlawing traditional religious practices while promoting Christian religious and educational programs, simply eroded much of the tribes' ability to govern. The cores of the tribal cultures were driven underground, and the BIA and Christian missionaries became the de facto governing forces on reservations.

In 1883, the Secretary of Interior established the Courts of Indian Offenses to replace tribal forums of justice. The purpose of these courts was to educate and "civilize" the tribes with the BIA and Congress providing the funding for the courts.[7] During this period, traditional tribal law was seriously weakened, losing its authority to a BIA legal system composed of the Indian

---

[2] See generally, Judith V. Royster, The Legacy of Allotment, 27 ARIZ. ST. L.J. 1 (1995).

[3] Act of Feb. 8, 1887, Ch. 119, 24 Stat. 388 (1887) (codified as amended at 25 U.S.C. §§ 331-34, 341-42, 348-49, 354, 381 (1983)).

[4] Steven Tyler, A History of Indian Policy 104 (1973).

[5] The Indian land base of 138 million acres at the enactment of the General Allotment Act of 1887 had been reduced to 48 million acres by enactment of the Indian Reorganization Act of 1934, which repudiated the allotment era policies. Felix S. Cohen, Handbook of Federal Indian Law 105-07 (1982 ed.). See also Royster, supra note 3.

[6] Charles F. Wilkinson, American Indians, Time and the Law 20 (1986).

[7] F. Cohen, Handbook of Federal Indian Law, 333 (1942 ed.).

agent, a code of Indian offenses, Indian police, and agency-appointed chiefs and judges.[8] Today, about twenty-two courts known as CFR courts (referring to the Code of Federal Regulations), are heirs to the Courts of Indian Offenses.[9] In 1885, Congress enacted the Major Crimes Act to extend federal court jurisdiction over felony criminal offenses committed by Indians on Indian reservations.[10] The overwhelming effect of the allotment period weakened the traditional tribal governments and law.

Alaska had its own allotment law, known as the Alaska Native Allotment Act (ANAA), to provide Alaska Natives with an opportunity to obtain individual title to land.[11] The Act was different than the General Allotment Act in that it was not intended to break up large reservation lands, but rather established a preference right to perfect legal title to the land Alaska Natives used and occupied. Thus, the Act gave Natives a preference right to perfect title to lands historically used by them, and to defeat homestead and other claims. The Act prevented continued loss of Native homelands since there were no reservations or ways to protect title to Native lands.

The Act, however, was not self-executing like the General Allotment Act, and the ANAA required individuals to file a written application and establish their use and occupancy. This bureaucratic process lent itself to abuse, rigorous factual proof for individuals, shifting BIA interpretations of legal and factual criteria, and due process violations. In 1980, Congress sought to eliminate some of the criteria in the passage of the Alaska National Interest Lands Conservation Act.[12] Numerous issues still remain with regard to allotments approved under the Act and are the focus of much litigation. Despite the Act being repealed the lands conveyed remain a focal point of the federal trust responsibility to Alaska Natives. Additionally, it has been repeatedly held in Alaska that the federal government has a fiduciary responsibility to administer these lands for the benefit of Alaska Natives.[13]

---

[8] Christine Zuni, Strengthening What Remains, 7 KAN. L.J. & PUB. POL'Y 17 (1997). Some Indian tribes were exempted from this system such as the Five Civilized Tribes – the Cherokees, Choctaws, Creeks, Chickasaws and Seminoles, and the Indians of New York, the Osage, the Pueblos of New Mexico and Arizona, and the Eastern Cherokee.

[9] The regulations that govern these courts are found at 25 C.F.R. Part 11, Law and Order on Indian Reservations (2002).

[10] 18 U.S.C. §§ 1153, 3242 (1984 & Supp. 1988). The Major Crimes Act was a Congressional reaction to the Supreme Court decision in *Ex Parte Crow Dog*, 109 U.S. 556 (1883), which reserved a lower court decision finding Crow Dog guilty of murdering another tribal member Spotted Tail. The tribal resolution and remedy included an ordered gift and reconciliation among the families, which was objected to by the non-Indian public. See Sidney L. Harring, Crow Dog's Case: American Indian Sovereignty, Tribal Law, and United States Law in the Nineteenth Century 10-12 (1994).

[11] Act of May 17, 1906, 34 Stat. 197, codified at 43 U.S.C. § 270-1 (1970). This Act was repealed under the Alaska Native Claims Settlement Act, 45 Stat. 710, 43 U.S.C. § 1617.

[12] Act of December 2, 1980, P.L. 96-487, 94 Stat.2371, codified in part of 16 and 43 U.S.C.

[13] See *Aguilar v. United States,* 474 F.Supp. 840 (D. AK. 1979), the preference right under the Act to Alaska Natives held sufficient to require the United States to recover lands for Native applicant if erroneously conveyed to another.

B. Indian Reorganization

In 1934, the federal government reversed its national policy to one of supporting tribal self-government when Congress passed the Indian Reorganization Act (IRA) of 1934.[14] Congress repudiated the policies of the allotment era, and attempted to encourage economic development, self-determination, cultural plurality, and the revival of tribalism.[15] The overriding purpose of the IRA was to establish a means to encourage and facilitate tribes to assume greater self-government, both politically and economically. The IRA provided tribes the opportunity to adopt their own constitutions and establish their own court systems to replace Courts of Indian Offenses. The Department of Interior provided tribes boilerplate versions of constitutions based upon the United States government model yet a tribe's version required Secretarial approval to become effective.[16] Not all tribes that organized under the IRA adopted constitutions, and a number of tribes did not organize under the IRA.[17]

As originally enacted, the IRA did not apply to Alaska. The IRA, however, was amended in 1936 to take into account the unique needs of Alaska Natives.[18] The Alaska amendments permitted the Secretary of Interior to designate "public lands which are actually occupied by Indians or Eskimos" either as new reservations or as additions to existing reservations.[19] Under this authority, the Secretary of Interior designated reservations for the Venetie, Karluk, Akutan, Diomede, Unalakleet, Wales and Hydaburg communities.[20] The amendment also permitted Alaska Natives to organize under federal constitutions and business charters, like the lower 48 tribes, if they had a "common bond of occupation, or association, or residence within a well defined neighborhood, community or rural district."[21] The amendment essentially addressed the issue of isolated rural Alaska Native villages and a few large reservations.

Criticisms of the IRA approach include the belief that the model constitutions and model codes for tribes limit criminal jurisdiction of tribal courts to minor offenses, subjected tribal laws and ordinances to Department of Interior approval, and limited the sentencing power of tribal courts to a maximum imprisonment period of six months for criminal offenses. Most of the tribal governments established under the IRA, unlike the federal and state governments, have no provision for separation of powers. The governing body is the tribal council, and in many instances, it performs both legislative and executive responsibilities. Furthermore, because the IRA governments rely on the European style of representative government through elections by

---

[14] 25 U.S.C §§ 461 – 94 (1983).

[15] See David H. Getches et al., Federal Indian Law: Cases and Materials 216-21 (3d ed. 1993).

[16] See 25 U.S.C. § 476.

[17] During the two year when the tribes could accept or reject the IRA, 258 elections were held. 181 tribes accepted the IRA, and 77 tribes rejected it. Getches, supra note 15 at 221.

[18] Act of May 1, 1936, 49 Stat. 1250, 25 U.S.C. § 473a.

[19] 25 U.S.C. § 496 (1970). This section was repealed by the Federal Land and Policy Management Act of 1976, sec. 703, 90 Stat. 2789.

[20] Hydaburg was held to be not properly established as a reserve under the IRA. *United States v. Libby, McNeil & Libby,* 107 F.ed Supp. 697 (D. Alaska 1952).

[21] 25 U.S.C. § 473a.

districts on the reservation as well as the use of English and the written word, the IRA has been perceived as an assault on traditional tribal governments. As a result, some IRA elected tribal governments are controversial[22] in that they operate to the exclusion of traditionalist interests and depart from consensus-based traditional government.[23]

On the other hand, the elimination of the absolute discretion exercised by the Interior Department in tribal internal affairs is considered a positive aspect of the IRA. Another by-product of the IRA was better control and management of tribal property. In other words, the IRA sought to end the paternalistic regime of the BIA superintendent and institute a more representative system to modify the control of the federal government. The experiences of IRA tribes and the powers exercised under the new "modern governments" vary as widely as the tribes themselves. Tribal governments achieved considerable revitalization during this era.

C. Termination

Beginning in the mid-1940s, the federal government began to move away from the IRA ideals and once again moved towards a complete integration of Indians into the general U.S. population. Congress unanimously voted to terminate the federal trust relationship with hundreds of tribes across the country and transfer jurisdiction over to the states. The policy was touted for ending federal supervision of Indian people and for rapidly assimilating tribes. Although termination has ended, it stands as a chilling reminder to Indian people that Congress can unilaterally decide to extinguish the special relationship the federal government has with tribes, without Indian consent.

During this period Congress passed "Public Law 280" in 1953. Public Law 280 was general legislation that extended state civil and criminal jurisdiction into Indian Country.[24] As originally enacted, Public Law 280 delegated jurisdiction over most crimes and many civil matters to six states: California, Nebraska, Minnesota (except for the Red Lake Reservation), Oregon (except for the Warm Springs Reservation), and Wisconsin (except for the Menominee Reservation). Alaska was included in this list in 1959 at the time of its statehood.[25] A total of sixteen states eventually became Public Law 280 states. The result of this law was unprecedented and served to limit the jurisdiction of tribal courts and increase state jurisdiction over Indians residing on reservations. In addition, other aspects of the federal termination program included transfer of educational responsibilities from the tribes and federal government to the states; the establishment of the Indian Claims Commission to hear and "wipe the slate clean" of violations of treaty provisions, land takings, etc, against the federal government[26]; and relocation programs to encourage Indians to leave the reservation and move to urban areas.

---

[22] See Getches, supra note 15 at 223-224.

[23] See Vine Deloria, Jr. & Clifford M. Lytle, American Indians, American Justice 15 (1983); Jerry Mander, In the Absence of the Sacred 279-83 (1991).

[24] 67 Stat.588 (1953).

[25] See Goldberg, Public Law 280, The Limits of State Jurisdiction Over Reservation Indians, 22 UCLA L.REV. 535 (1975).

[26] The Indian Claims Commission Act of 1946, 25 U.S.C. §§ 70 – 70V (1984), established a three member commission to adjudicate Indian claims against the United States.

D.   Self-Determination

Ironically, termination-- which was designed to once and for all detribalize Indians-- produced the opposite effect. The threat of termination galvanized tribes nationally to protest the congressional move towards termination and resulted in the establishment of national Indian organizations such as the National Congress of American Indians, National Indian Youth Council, and National Tribal Chairman Association. In the 1960's, federal policy entered a period of gradual transformation. In 1970, President Richard Nixon issued a landmark message to Congress calling for a new federal policy of self-determination for Indian nations. Under this policy, tribal governments grew increasingly sophisticated and were able, for the first time, to deliver meaningful governmental services to their people.

This policy of self-determination was supported by legislation such as the Indian Self-Determination and Education Assistance Act of 1975.[27] The Act expressly authorizes the Secretary of Interior and Health and Human Services to contract with, and make grants to, tribes and other tribal organizations for the delivery of services. The Act marked a fundamental change in philosophy concerning the administration of tribal affairs – the federal government funds tribal programs, but the programs are planned and administered by the tribes themselves. Beginning in the 1970's, there has been an unprecedented volume of tribal legislation, most favorable to tribal interests and supported by tribes. In most instances, Alaska Natives are included in this legislation to receive and participate in federal programs.

The federal legislation incorporates tribal governments as permanent players in the federal system. In 1968, the Indian Civil Rights Act (ICRA) was passed and the federal policy of recognizing tribal powers of self-government, including the authority to establish court systems for administering justice, was once again reaffirmed. While supporting tribal autonomy, the ICRA required tribal governments to adhere to most of the requirements of the Bill of Rights.[28]

Today, federal legislation continues to support tribal self-government, increased funding for court operations, other dispute resolution systems, and environmental programs. Enacted in 1993, the Indian Tribal Justice Act focuses on the development and improvement of tribal court systems as a whole.[29] The Act provides funding to tribal judicial systems, training programs for court personnel, and established an Office of Tribal Justice to handle funding to tribes and to promote cooperation between tribal, state and federal courts.[30] Tribal institutions are in a period of rapid growth and development. The number of tribal courts is increasing while training and financial support have bolstered confidence in, and support of, the tribal systems.

---

[27] 25 U.S.C. §§ 450a – 450m (1984).

[28] 25 U.S.C. §§ 1301 – 41 (1988).

[29] Public L. No. 103-176, 107 Stat. 2004 (1993) (codified as amended at 25 U.S.C. § 3601 (1994)).

[30] See Diana B. Garonzik, Full Reciprocity for Tribal Courts from a Federal Court Perspective: A proposed Amendment to the Full Faith and Credit Act, 45 EMORY L.J. 723, 747-48 (1996).

E. Alaska Native Claims Settlement Act of 1971

In 1971, Congress enacted the Alaska Native Claims Settlement Act (ANCSA), a major piece of federal legislation impacting the legal status and land ownership rights of Alaska Natives. Today, this complex legislation is essential to any discussion of Alaska Natives issues. In ANCSA, the tribes relinquished aboriginal claims to most of the state affecting 365 million acres.[31] In return, Alaska Natives agreed to receive land selection rights to 44 million acres along with monetary payments. Tribes with governmental powers did not receive the land title. Instead, the land was conveyed to Native Corporations – which Congress mandated were to be formed under Alaska state corporations laws. Twelve Regional Corporations own the subsurface land title, which includes mineral development rights for oil, coal, natural gas, gravel, etc. ANCSA also recognized 210 Native Village Corporations, which received surface estate title. Of the 210 Native Villages, approximately 120 are organized as municipalities under state law. Of those 120 Native villages, 70 are organized under the Indian Reorganization Act. The remaining ninety Alaska Native communities are governed solely by traditional village councils.[32]

There is a major distinction between the lower 48 tribes and the tribes in Alaska – there are no longer any reservations in Alaska (except for one – Annette Island) following the passage of ANCSA. Most of the land transferred to Natives under ANCSA is owned by the Native Regional and Village Corporations, most of which do not exercise tribal governmental functions. There are however, a few Alaska Native Villages that are considered federally- recognized tribes and hold some land. In 1998, the United States Supreme Court interpreted ANCSA to limit the territorial jurisdiction of Alaska Native tribes.[33] In *Alaska v. Native Village of Venetie Tribal Government*, the Court held that the tribe's former reservation is not considered "Indian country." This decision limited tribal authority to enact and impose a business activity tax upon private contractor, who was not a member of the tribe. This decision raises issues regarding the authority of tribes to exercise environmental regulatory jurisdiction on their lands over non-members.

Moreover, the *Venetie* decision made it clear that land conveyed to the Native Regional and Village Corporations under ANCSA is not "Indian Country". In Alaska, because the Regional and Village Corporations, for the most part, are private corporations which own their lands separately from the federally recognized tribes, there are open legal questions about the power of the local tribe to exercise environmental jurisdiction over Native Corporation lands.[34]

F. The Federal Trust Responsibility to Tribes

Tribes in the United States, unlike any other indigenous group in the world, have significant standing because they have a trust relationship with the federal government

---

[31] David H. Getches et al., Federal Indian Law: Cases and Materials 907 (4th ed. 1998).

[32] See David S. Case, Alaska Natives and American Laws 373-78 (Rev. ed. 1984).

[33] *Alaska v. Native Village of Venetie Tribal Government*, 522 U.S. 520 (1998).

[34] IPS would like to thank Alma Upicksoun, Vice President and General Counsel of the Arctic Slope Regional Corporation, for her review and comments on this section relating to ANCSA.

established by judicial decisions, treaties, agreements and federal laws that set forth certain obligations, commitments, and guarantees for tribal homelands, tribal people, and tribal resources. The courts, Congress, and the Executive Branch have recognized the trust responsibility of the United States throughout the span of federal Indian law.[35]

The foundation of the trusteeship of the federal government to Indian tribes is traceable to the first cessions of Indian lands to the federal government. The promises made by the United States in exchange for millions of acres of tribal land impose on the federal government "moral obligations of the highest responsibility and trust."[36] This principle that the federal government has a duty to keep its word and fulfill its promises to tribes is known as the "doctrine of trust responsibility." Most fundamentally, the modern form of the federal government's trust obligation is the "duty to protect [tribal] separatism by protecting tribal lands, resources, and the native way of life."[37]

The Supreme Court has made clear that in administering Indian trust property or trust money, the United States is a trustee, subject to the fiduciary duties attendant to a trust relationship.[38] The Government's trust obligations arise whenever the United States exercises control over, or management of, the trust property of Indian tribes and individual Indians. The courts have held federal officials to "moral obligations of the highest responsibility and trust" and "the most exacting fiduciary standards,"[39] and to be "bound by every moral and equitable consideration to discharge its trust with good faith and fairness."[40]

Each federal agency, including EPA, is bound by this trust responsibility. The EPA 1984 Indian Policy states: "[I]n keeping with the federal trust responsibility, [EPA] will assure that tribal concerns and interests are considered whenever EPA's actions and/or decisions may affect reservation environments . . . [T]he Agency will endeavor to protect the environmental interest of Indian Tribes when carrying out its responsibilities that may affect the reservations."[41] This Indian Policy has been reaffirmed by subsequent EPA Administrators.

The IPS notes that EPA's policies have been primarily aimed at assisting tribes in regulating activities on their own reservations. EPA has not taken an active stance on pollution

---

[35] For a general discussion of the trust doctrine see Felix S. Cohen, HANDBOOK OF FEDERAL INDIAN LAW 220-28 (Rennard Strickland et al, eds. 3d ed. 1982). See also Mary C. Woods, Indian Lands and the Promise of Native Sovereignty: The Trust Doctrine Revisited, UTAH LAW REV. 1471, 1496-97 (1994).

[36] *Seminole Nation v. United States,* 316 U.S. 286, 296-97 (1942). See also *United States v. Mason,* 412 U.S. 391, 397 (1973).

[37] Wood, supra note 35 at 1496, and footnote citing *Northern Arapahoe Tribe v. Hodel,* 808 F.2d 741, 750 (10th Cir. 1987) (finding trust duty to protect tribe's wildlife resources).

[38] *United States v, Mitchell,* 463 U.S. 206, 225 (1983).

[39] *Seminole Nation v. United States, supra* note 36 at 297.

[40] *United States v. Payne,* 264 U.S. 446, 448 (1924).

[41] U.S. Environmental Protection Agency, EPA Policy For The Administration of Environmental Programs on Indian Reservations (Nov. 8, 1984).

affecting reservation environments[42] or tribal risks associated with transboundary pollution of tribal use of water and wildlife.[43] The IPS calls upon EPA to address the ever-present contamination occurring on American Indian and Alaska Native lands, and to seek ways to assist in the protection of tribal homelands. Additionally, EPA must remember that tribes are not merely another community or stakeholder group. EPA has a duty and obligation to protect and preserve tribal and Alaska Native lands, and to ensure that the best interests of tribal governments and Alaska Natives are not harmed or subordinated to the trustee's own interests. Accordingly, the IPS cautions the EPA to consider and implement its Charge judiciously to ensure that its focus of public participation and due process by tribal governments does not conflict with or interfere with its protection of tribal rights and Indian self-determination.

G. Environmental Jurisdiction on Tribal Lands

The fundamental notions of tribal sovereignty relevant to pollution control are: dominion over the territory of the reservation, sovereignty over citizens of the tribe, the right to make and enforce laws and domestic policy, and control of the natural resources, including the reservation environment. In earlier times, a tribe's inherent authority to exercise jurisdiction throughout its territory was nearly complete and unchallenged. The federal allotment policy of creating checkerboard land base on some reservations has made the assertion of tribal authority more complex. In this respect, the early federal policies continue to affect tribal sovereignty and inform the interpretation and application of the law in Indian country.

Indian tribal sovereignty remains a doctrine of considerable vitality because of its internal significance to tribal governments and the resulting external consequences for the states and non-Indians within Indian country. Black's Law Dictionary defines "sovereignty" as "the supreme, absolute, and uncontrollable power by which any independent state is governed."[44] Today, tribes continue to exercise their sovereignty over their territory involving a wide range of governmental functions, but still face many threats to their reservation environments. Through the exercise of their sovereignty, tribes seek to address the contamination and pollution impacting their communities.

1. Development Impacting Indian Lands

There are over 560 federally recognized Indian tribes in the United States.[45] Indian tribes and individual tribal members own approximately 56.6 million acres of land, an increase of more

---

[42] See *Blue Legs v. United States Bureau of Indian Affairs,* 867 F.2d 1094 (8th Cir. 1989).

[43] A 1991 EPA Concept Paper opts for a consensual approach on transboundary pollution issues involving tribal and state governments, and recommends that EPA will act as a moderator for discussion rather than acting as trustee for the tribes in protection their resources. U.S. Environmental Protection Agency, Federal and State Roles in Protection and Regulation of Reservation Environments (1991).

[44] Black's Law Dictionary 1568, 4th ed. Rev. (West Publishing Co. 1968).

[45] Getches, supra note 15 at 8. Not all native nations are federally recognized.

than 4 million acres since 1980.[46] Half of the 1.9 million American Indians live on or adjacent to one of 310 reservations.[47] Today, reservations contain one or more of three types of land tenure: (1) tribally owned land held in trust by the federal government; (2) allotted lands owned by individual Indians held in trust by the federal government; and (3) parcels of land owned in fee simple, usually by non-Indians, as a result of the federal Allotment policy.

The BIA continues to exercise broad discretion in dealing with Indian governments. Federal statues, as well as the day-to-day supervision over land and resource development on reservations, grant the BIA substantial involvement over timber, mineral, agricultural and range resource development. The BIA participates in resource negotiations, oversees contracts and leases, and collects royalties and payments on resources. At times, BIA's decisions relating to the economic development of tribal resources are controversial, and often times receive criticism for not being in the best interests of the tribe and/or individual tribal members.

In addition to the BIA, other federal agencies including the Bureau of Land Management, Department of Energy, Bureau of Reclamation, and the Corp of Engineers, make decisions impacting tribal lands and resources, either on-reservation or off-reservation. These decisions often impact lands where tribes exercise their subsistence rights of hunting, fishing and gathering. The lands often contain valuable cultural resources such as sacred and spiritual sites for tribes. The lands, too, have been polluted, and tribes must develop ways to protect these natural and cultural resources.

Corporation pressure to develop reservation resources has often been overwhelming and damaging to reservation environments. In some leases and contracts signed by some tribal leadership and the BIA in the 1950's, devastating consequences have resulted which affect the tribes today. Tribes and individual tribal members lease their lands to non-Indians for grazing, mining, commercial and residential purposes. Most leased rangeland is seriously overgrazed. Reservations have been mined for coal and uranium, and many of these operations have left a barren landscape with lethal contamination impacting the health of tribal people, water, soils and air.[48] In addition, the BIA's past timber clear cutting practices have led to the near decimation of tribal forest, wildlife, and fishery resources. Consequently, the past exploitation of tribal resources has severely impacted tribal traditional economies and way of life. Certainly, the use of tribal lands and resources might have resulted in short term benefits, but they have also had

---

[46] *Id.* at 20. Nearly all the land held is trust by the federal government for the tribes or their individual members. *Id.* at 21. Another 44 million acres are owned by Alaska Natives pursuant to the Alaska Native Claims Settlement Act. *Id.* at 20.

[47] *Id.* at 8, 13, 15.

[48] See Winona LaDuke, Environmental Work: An Indigenous Perspective, 8 N.E. Indian Q. 16, 17 (1991); See also Mary Christine Wood, Protecting the Attributes of Native Sovereignty: A New Trust Paradigm for Federal Actions Affecting Tribal Lands and Resources, 1995 UTAH L. REV. 109, 166-67.

profound long-term ecological and cultural consequences. Today, tribes have to confront the severe environmental problems resulting from these activities.[49]

Currently, some tribal governments continue to receive intense pressure to develop and industrialize their reservation lands. Many tribes have tribal corporations, created under the IRA, poised to enter into economic ventures with outside industry. Many tribal members oppose the use of their lands for non-Indian development, mining, and waste disposal, and have challenged tribal council efforts to approve such ventures. Thus, tribal governments must address the continuing tension between building strong economies to meet mounting tribal social needs, and ensuring that the natural resources are not overexploited and the reservation environment and land base remain viable for future generations. "Managing" the environment to increase productivity or to restore or preserve the environmental norms will have enormous future consequences for tribal communities.

2.   Tribes as Sovereign Nations – Protecting Tribal Homelands

Tribal authority to regulate in Indian Country arises from the inherent sovereign powers of Indian tribes, which were self-governing nations for centuries before the European nations arrived on this continent. The three branches of the United States have continually recognized Indian tribes as politically distinct nations possessing inherent sovereign powers. In the early 1800's, in a trilogy of foundation Indian law cases, Supreme Court Chief Justice John Marshall established that Indian tribes possessed powers of inherent sovereignty that arise from tribes' status as independent nations before and at the time of European arrival.[50] Felix Cohen, the prominent master of Indian law, wrote in his treatise on Indian law:

> Perhaps the most basic principles of all Indian law, supported by a host of decisions hereafter analyzed, is the principle that those powers which are lawfully vested in an Indian tribe are not, in general, delegated powers granted by express acts of Congress, but rather inherent powers of a limited sovereignty which has never been extinguished. Each Indian tribe begins its relationship with the Federal Government as a sovereign power, recognized as such in treaty and legislation.[51]

Tribes are considered sovereign, completely separate from state and federal governments, in the sense that tribal sovereign powers derive from the consent of separate peoples whose governments were established prior to European arrival. Since tribal governments predate the formation of the state and federal governments and are not derived from, or the provisions of the

---

[49] See Ward Churchill and Winona LaDuke, Native North America: The Political Economy of Radioactive Colonialism, The State of Native America: Genocide, Colonization, and Resistence 241, 244-55 (M. Annette Jaimes, ed., 1992).

[50] *Johnson v. McIntosh,* 21 U.S. (8 Wheat.) 543, 547 (1832); *Cherokee Nation v. Georgia,* 30 U.S. (5 Pet.) 1, 17 (1831); *Worcester v. Georgia,* 31 U.S. (6 Pet.) 515 (1832).

[51] Felix Cohen, Handbook of Federal Indian Law, 122 (1942 ed.).

federal constitution do not bind dependent upon the federal constitution, tribal governments.[52] Today, fully functioning Indian nations embody sovereignty comprised of at least four distinct, yet interwoven attributes: secure land bases, functioning economies, self-government, and cultural vitality. Some commentators describe these attributes as geographic and political separation. The tribes' continued existence and autonomy depends on maintaining all four of these attributes of sovereignty.

The responsibility of a sovereign is three fold – the ability to govern its own members, a territorial component and the exclusion of competing sovereigns. One of the most basic powers of a sovereign people is the power to select their form of government.[53] Tribes have chosen to adopt their form of self-government in accordance with their political and cultural history. Many tribes have chosen to adopt a government model similar to the United States. Others have chosen to retain their traditional forms of government. And, on some reservations, there exist IRA governments and traditional governments, which creates conflict on some issues relating to governance.

As sovereign governments, Indian nations generally have the inherent civil authority to maintain law and order by enacting laws governing the conduct of persons, both Indian and non-Indians, within reservations[54]; to enforce and administer justice by establishing bodies, such as tribal law enforcement and courts[55]; and to regulate the conduct of non-members who enter consensual relationships with the tribe or its members and whose conduct threatens or directly affects a significant tribal interest, economic security, or health and general welfare of the tribe.[56] These civil powers are exercised by most tribes in the United States, as determined by each tribal government. Importantly, these inherent rights and powers are retained unless they have been given up by a tribe pursuant to a treaty, agreement, tribal constitution, or limited by a congressional act.[57] Tribes, however, do not retain inherent criminal jurisdiction over non-Indians on reservations,[58] but do retain jurisdiction over non-member Indians.[59]

In earlier times, a tribe's inherent authority to exercise jurisdiction throughout its territory was nearly complete and unchallenged. Today, however, tribal authority over non-Indians

---

[52] See *Santa Clara Pueblo v. Martinez,* 436 U.S. 49, 56 (1978) ("as separate sovereigns pre-existing the Constitution, tribes have historically been regarded as unconstrained by those constitutional provisions framed specifically for limitations on federal or state authority.").

[53] *Id.* at 55.

[54] *United States v. Wheeler,* 435 U.S. 313 (1978).

[55] *Williams v. Lee,* 358 U.S. 217 (1959).

[56] *Montana v. United States,* 450 U.S. 544, 565-566 (1981).

[57] *Menominee Tribe v. United States,* 391 U.S. 404 (1968); *United States v. Dion,* 476 U.S. 734, 739 (1986). This is a fundamental principle of Indian law known as the reserved rights doctrine.

[58] *Oliphnat v. Suquamish Indian Tribe,* 435 U.S. 191 (1978).

[59] *Duro v. Reina,* 495 U.S. 676 (1990); See also *United States v. Lara,* 541 U.S. ___, 124 S.Ct. 1628 (2004). The United States Supreme Court in Lara specifically recognized the continuing viability of the inherent sovereignty of Tribal governments. The Court held that the inherent authority of tribes has never been extinguished and that it was only limited when executed in a manner inconsistent with federal law and policy.

within its territory is more complex. Accordingly, despite being in the era of tribal self-determination, the Supreme Court decisions on the exercise of tribal authority over their territory have been moving in the opposite direction. By finding that tribal sovereignty over non-Indians in tribal communities is inconsistent with tribes' "dependent status," these decisions are reshaping and diminishing tribal rights and undermining federal Indian policy.[60] The trend of the Supreme Court towards promoting the notion that tribes do not have the inherent authority to regulate non-Indian activities impacting the political integrity and general welfare of the tribes raises serious concerns about the future erosion of tribal sovereignty in the context of environmental regulation. It is difficult to overstate the change in the law that has occurred regarding tribal jurisdiction over non-Indians during the past 25 years by the Supreme Court. EPA must be ever mindful of these changes in the law and the treatment of non-Indians who reside within tribal territories.[61]

The new restrictions on tribal power represent a judicial trend only; they have not been paralleled by any changes in the congressional and executive policies concerning Indian affairs. Certainly, if the tribal exercise of environmental authority are delegated under federal law, rather than based on inherent tribal authority, tribes may have a stronger argument to exert such authority. Implementing an authorized federal environmental program, for example, includes the capacity to comprehend and respond to concerns, needs and priorities of tribal members and non-members living on the reservation. Providing an opportunity for public participation can strengthen tribal government and sovereignty, and alter in a positive way the tribes' relations with the rest of the community and off-reservation communities. With the support of the community, and recognition of the tribal environmental programs, a tribe can more effectively exercise its sovereign authority, and expect less interference in its internal affairs. In turn, the tribe is better able to protect and preserve its homeland.

In addition to a tribe's inherent sovereign authority, a tribal nation may assume regulatory authority under delegation of federal powers. Where Congress delegates its federal authority to tribes, it is to governments possessing independent powers, particularly over internal and social affairs. For tribal governments, these sovereign powers are critical to ensuring that a reservation's pollution sources are regulated and managed properly, to preserve the tribal homelands reserved under treaties. The quality of the reservation environment relates directly to the economic security and health and welfare of a tribal community.

---

[60] See David H. Getches, Beyond Indian Law: The Rehnquist Court's Pursuit of States' Rights, Color-Blind Justice and Mainstream Values, 86 MINN.L.REV. 267 (2001).

[61] In *Nevada v. Hicks,* 533 U.S. 353 (2001), the Supreme Court held that tribes have no power to regulate the activities of state law enforcement officers executing a search warrant against an Indian on tribal land within a reservation. The expansive rationale of *Hicks* represents an astonishing diminution in the control that tribes may exercise over their own reservation. Additionally, in *Atkinson Trading Post Company v. Shirley,* 532 U.S. 645 (2001), the Supreme Court held that the Navajo Nation lacked authority to impose a hotel occupancy tax on a hotel owned by a non-Indian.

In 1984, the EPA adopted a "Policy for the Administration of Environmental Programs on Indian Reservations,"[62] in which it recognized tribal governments as the appropriate non-federal parties for "setting standards, making environmental policy decisions and managing programs on reservations, consistent with Agency standards and regulations."[63] On July 11, 2001, the EPA Administrator affirmed the Bush Administration's adoption of the "EPA Policy for the Administration of Environmental Programs on Indian Reservations." This Policy affirms the long-standing federal principles of Indian self-determination and the government-to-government relationship between tribes and the federal government and applies them to the area of environmental regulatory programming. The principles of EPA's Policy treat Indian reservations as coherent units, within which tribal governments are recognized as the appropriate entities to set and enforce environmental standards on reservations to protect human health and the environment.

Additionally, Congress has expressly authorized EPA to treat tribal governments in the same manner as states, giving tribes a major role in the administration of federal environmental programs and eligibility for grants and contracts. Congress has amended many of the federal environmental laws consistent with the 1984 EPA Indian Policy to include provisions in the Clean Air Act[64]; the Clean Water Act[65]; the Safe Drinking Water Act[66]: and the Comprehensive Environmental Response, Compensation and Liability Act (Superfund Act), to recognize tribes as controlling governments, to receive grants for pollution control, and to set standards and enforce certain standards. Consistent with EPA's Indian Policy, Congress also views the political boundaries of the reservation as delineating the appropriate regulatory area for management of environmental programs. The Federal Insecticide Fungicide and Rodenticide Act (FIFRA) expressly permits EPA to enter into cooperative agreements with tribes to enforce pesticide use violations and to train and certify pesticides applicators, but does not expressly contain a treatment as state section. The Resource Conservation and Recovery Act (RCRA) is the only federal environmental law that does not allow tribes to be authorized to run the federal program, as determined in a federal court case.

These changes in the federal law present tribal governments with an opportunity and challenge to establish environmental programs that protect public health and the environment, and provide for sustainable economic development. Tribes are seeking to preserve the quality of their reservation environments for present and future generations of tribal members and to protect and restore the natural environments that sustain tribal cultures. Many tribes have made substantial progress and are building effective environmental protection regulatory programs.

---

[62] Supra note 40.

[63] *Id.* See also EPA's accompanying legal analysis to its 1991 Policy Statement, Regulatory Jurisdiction of Indian Tribes, 56 Fed. Reg. 64876 (Dec. 12, 1991).

[64] 42 U.S.C. §§ 7401 – 7642.

[65] 33 U.S.C. §§ 1251- 1377.

[66] 42 U.S.C. § 300(f)(j).

Providing for Meaningful Involvement and Fair Treatment

I.   Purposes for Providing Meaningful Involvement and Fair Treatments

At the time a tribe assumes authorization to develop and implement a federal environmental program, the tribal environmental program should simultaneously work to develop processes to provide for meaningful involvement and fair treatment.   Many tribal programs have assumed these obligations and have promulgated rules, regulations, and policies; established standards; issued or denied permits for proposed activities with full public participation and due process; and have taken compliance and enforcement actions against violators of environmental laws.   In addition to federal law requirements for public participation and due process, there are sound policy reasons that support these principles.   In this Appendix, the IPS presents three related reasons or perspectives to support the development of public participation and due process procedures, including (1) promoting good governance; (2) respecting interests of community members; and (3) protecting and promoting tribal sovereignty. The IPS provides these perspectives to EPA to help articulate to tribal governments the importance of, and legal requirements for, providing meaningful involvement and fair treatment when developing and implementing federal environmental programs.

A.   Providing Good Governance

Governments have a broad set of responsibilities including protecting the health and safety of its citizens or members, improving the community's quality of life through education, planning, property protection, and securing a viable economic future.   With this wide range of responsibilities, governments are frequently tasked with balancing competing interests. Governments often mediate conflicts between those who are concerned with protecting the environment and those seeking to ensure long-term economic stability, or between individual interests and the interest of the greater community.   To be credible, government officials must demonstrate transparency in their decision-making.

The fundamental exercise of sovereignty by a government includes not only power, but also the responsibility to establish a governmental infrastructure and institutions that provide for sound decision-making. It also requires the implementation of the laws and regulations in a manner that recognizes the interests of its citizenry, and in the case of tribal governments, tribal members and non-members residing on the reservation.   Good governance informs the community, educates its citizens, builds public trust, and seeks to improve both the citizens' and community's quality of life.   Responsive government also includes the capacity to comprehend and respond to the individual community member's needs and priorities and to mediate conflicts within the community through an established process.

Providing opportunities for public participation can strengthen tribal government and sovereignty and improve the tribes' relations with the rest of the community and off-reservation communities.   Support from the community, by recognizing the legitimacy of tribal institutions, increases a tribe's ability to exercise its sovereignty and authority and will likely result in less interference from external parties. In turn, a tribe is better able to protect and preserve its resources, land base and homeland.

B.   Respecting the Interests of Community Members

Tribal environmental program decisions affect the entire social, cultural and spiritual beliefs as well as the political fabric of a community because such decisions impact the communal rights to live on, use, harvest, conserve, and transfer lands within the reservation, and the land, itself, as community. Accordingly, tribal members have a legitimate stake in the decisions affecting the environment and land base in which they hold a communal interest. Indeed, on many reservations, individual tribal members own a majority of the land base as a result of the allotment era. Moreover, communal ownership and kinship places certain duties and responsibilities on some tribal members with respect to the land and resources, and to all the living beings of the environment. Tribal leaders, in addressing the myriad of important issues pertaining to running a government, must also be cognizant of the traditional tribal values of respect, reciprocity, humility and connectedness as these relate to land and tribal members. Often, certain individuals and traditional and religious tribal leaders advocate the importance of cultural integrities to preserve the beauty and stability of the community, to protect the health and welfare of the residents, and to plan for future generations. These voices, comments, and opinions serve an important role in the tribal institutional setting.

Tribal leadership often calls upon federal agencies to recognize tribal interests and to consult with them on federal decisions based upon the trust obligations owed to tribes. Similarly, tribal members request their tribal leadership to recognize, as many tribal leaders do, the responsibilities they have to the membership, such as informing the membership of proposed tribal government actions and enabling the membership to voice an opinion in support or in opposition to governmental decision-making impacting their rights, natural resources, welfare, and lives. Community interests do not always expect to get all they want, but they do expect to be heard, to be taken seriously, and to be informed of government decisions and processes

Given the history of neglect by the federal government in protecting tribal land bases, waters, soils, air, and placing the health of tribal members at risk for cancers, birth defects, higher rates of respiratory problems and immune deficiency diseases, tribal community members are keenly aware of the long-term consequences of uninformed decision-making and over-exploiting resources. Indeed, the impetus for establishing a tribal environmental program is to clean up contamination, confront ecological degradation, and seek to improve the overall quality of life for tribal community members.

Tribal decision-making seeks to reflect the history, experience, culture and wishes of the unique people and community it serves. Tribal members share common culture, customs, traditions, kinships and history with the tribal leadership that is elected or appointed as part of the established tribal government. Traditionally, tribal decisions were not taken lightly in Indian societies, but were carefully deliberated. As part of this deliberative process, tribal institutions should seek out comments and opinions of elders, cultural committees, individuals impacted, and the community as a whole.

Importantly, the federal policies of assimilation and allotment have been abandoned, but their legacy remains. One feature of this legacy, on many reservations, is a large population of non-member landowners, who are either members of other tribes or non-tribal. Also, non-tribally-owned businesses and industry have been doing business on some reservation for many years, prior to tribes establishing environmental programs. Tribal governments face the challenge of how to accommodate the interests and rights of non-members, while still exercising tribal self-government.

Certainly, tribal governments are the ultimate decision-makers on these issues and it is not the intent of the IPS to advocate for the wholesale reflection of a set of European principles in a tribal context. In short, the IPS acknowledges the tension between borrowing familiar principles of United States constitutional law and permitting Indian people the freedom and dignity to govern themselves according to their own vision. Tribal Councilmember of the Pueblo of Laguna, Frank Cerno, shared the following:

> [T]here is vision that all tribes share that is one of continuing on for generations to come, with the idea in mind that we have survived for all these years, under some very adverse circumstances, and that we will continue to survive, but only if we dream things that can definitely become reality.
>
> * * *
>
> Vision is the ability to dream things that never were and bring them to reality; the ability to clearly set out goals and objectives that will produce the framework for accomplishing that vision; and the ability to bring the necessary resources to bear on the further development of that dream.
>
> Vision is foresightedness; the ability to bring together diverse thoughts on diverse issues culminating in a plan of action, recognizing the past, building upon the present, for the purpose of securing the future.
>
> It isn't that what we as tribal leaders, in tribal government, are all about, making sure that we can 'secure the future' for our younger generations to come.[1]

C. Protecting and Promoting Tribal Sovereignty

Tribal sovereign autonomy and self-government, a principled foundation for Indian law, has weathered over 150 years of U.S. jurisprudence,[2] and indeed, insulating tribes against the passage of time is a consistent theme in the law. Tribal separatism remains both a focal point for

---

[1] Pueblo of Laguna Comments on Preliminary Draft on the Meaningful Involvement and Fair Treatment by Tribal Environmental Regulatory Programs 4, April 2, 2004.

[2] Charles F. Wilkinson, American Indians, Time and the Law 122 (1986).

modern Indian policy[3] and for tribes themselves. A priority implicit in tribal separatism is maintaining a homeland in which both present and future generations of the tribe may live. A viable tribal land base is the linchpin to other attributes of sovereignty. The tribal territory forms the geographical limits of the tribe's jurisdiction, supports a residing population, is the basis of the tribal economy, and provides an irreplaceable place for cultural traditions often premised on the sacredness of land. Through control over Indian lands and resources, Indian nations maintain a degree of economic self-sufficiency necessary to Indian self-determination. Justice Black once observed the attachment that tribal people have to their established homelands as follows:

> It may be hard for us to understand why these Indians cling so tenaciously to their lands and traditional way of life. The record does not leave the impression that the lands of their reservation are the most fertile, the landscape the most beautiful or their homes the most splendid specimens of architecture. But this is their home – their ancestral home. There, they, their children, and their forebears were born. They, too, have their memories and their loves. Some things are worth more than money and the costs of a new enterprise.[4]

Land will always occupy an important place in Indian cultures. Accordingly, tribes have a vital stake in resource and environmental management to preserve their homelands and their sovereignty.

Similarly, tribes should be aware of public perceptions about the role of tribal government in providing fundamental fairness to all residents of the reservation. To many non-Indians, the reservation remains a foreign place and the governmental structure is a mystery. Some states voice concerns about law and order and the efficiency of government. There are also questions about the ability of tribal governments to guarantee due process and fairness. Many of these criticisms are based upon a lack of knowledge and understanding of the structures of tribal governments, anecdotal evidence, unwillingness to recognize tribal institutions, and outright prejudice. Whether they are unfounded or not, the public and community perception of tribal institutions and their environmental programs should be recognized by tribal governments, and tribes should work to address these misconceptions.

Some of these same concerns were leveled at tribal courts in a 1978 report, developed by the National American Indian Court Judges Association that assessed the strengths and weaknesses of tribal courts.[5] The Judges Association describes serious problems with political interference, inadequate tribal laws, and a tendency toward summary judgment when defense counsel was absent. However, the Association also found many strengths in the tribal court

---

[3] See, Indian Self-Determination and Education Act, 25 U.S.C. §§ 450a – 450m (1984); Wilkinson, supra note 2 at 122.

[4] *Federal Power Comm'n v. Tuscarora Indian Nation,* 362 U.S. 99, 142 (1960) (Black, J., dissenting) (footnote omitted).

[5] The National American Indian Court of Judges Association, Indian Courts and the Future (1978).

system, including quick access to a fair forum, the ability to bridge the gap between law and Indian culture, a dedicated judiciary, and increased respect from federal courts, agencies and tribal governments. The recommendations included professional training for judges, enhanced funding for facilities and equipment, and insulation of tribal courts from political pressures. Since 1978, Congress has provided substantial appropriations directly to tribal courts to address their infrastructure building needs, training for staff with federal courts, and law and order code drafting. This assistance has greatly improved the administration of justice throughout Indian country. Moreover, some commentators have found that tribal courts are no less protective and much more accessible than federal courts have been in protecting civil rights on Indian reservations.[6]

The improvement of tribal courts over the years, is an example of the effective tribal institution building that has taken place on many reservations to address criticisms and to ensure that justice is accessible and afforded to all. Tribal environmental programs can deal with these similar criticisms by guaranteeing public participation and basic due process in their ordinances, rulemaking and administrative procedures. Building expertise, resources and community support can enhance the tribal goals. Tribal education of the public about the tribal process and institutions is a necessary step.

Institutional support needs to come from both the Indian and non-Indian communities and the regulated industry. Non-Indian companies who pursue mineral or other natural resource development affecting the tribal environment are accustomed to deriving some regulatory certainty from written laws and regulations. The establishment of advisory committees or boards can also lend support for a fair and meaningful system. Dialogue among the tribes and industry can foster mutual understanding of the need to define and make known specific environmental concerns. Importantly, these forms of public involvement enable the tribes to obtain sound input and receive information that can assist the tribe in its thoughtful deliberations and decision-making. A structured process can instill a careful weighing of concerns and issues by tribal program officers, council members, and community members. This approach is similar to traditional processes. Some tribes have already instituted these types of measures to defray the disapproval of, and challenges to, tribal authority.

---

[6] See Robert J. McCarthy, Civil Rights in Tribal Courts: The Indian Bill of Rights at Thirty Years, 34 IDAHO L.REV. 465 (1998). See also Juliana C. Repp, The Indian Civil Rights Act Tribal Constitutions and Tribal Courts, 16th Annual University of Washington Law School Indian Law Symposium, September 2003.

Glossary

Allotment: Surveyed reservation land distributed by the government to individual Indians under the provisions of the Dawes Allotment Act. Generally, 160 acres were allotted to heads of families; 80 acres to single persons; and 40 acres to other family members.

Bureau of Indian Affairs (BIA): Agency within the U.S. Department of the Interior responsible for administering the U.S. government's relationships with Indian governments and for overseeing Congress's trust responsibility for Indian lands and existence.

Consultation: A collaborative process between government peers resulting in a consensus on how to proceed.

Council: A group elected or appointed as an advisory or legislative body; council members are usually equal in power and authority.

Culture: The ideas, customs, skills, arts, etc., of a given people in a given period.

Cultural Resources: Places of historic significance, archeological sites and resources, graves and funery objects; also includes "traditional cultural properties" (see below).

Environmental Justice: Originating from a presidential executive order (#12898) environmental justice is the fair treatment and meaningful involvement of all people regardless of race, color, national origin, or income with respect to the development, implementation and enforcement of environmental laws, regulations and policies. Fair treatment also means that no group of people, including racial, ethnic or socioeconomic group should bear a disproportionate share of the negative environmental consequences resulting from industrial, municipal and commercial operations or the execution of federal, state, local and tribal programs and policies.

Environmental Protection Agency (EPA): EPA is a federal agency whose mission is "to protect human health and to safeguard the natural environment – air, water and land – upon which life depends. The Administrator of EPA reports directly to the President of the United States.

EPA Policy on Environmental Programs on Indian Reservations: In 1984, EPA was the first federal agency outside the Department of the Interior to adopt a formal policy statement regarding Indian Tribes. This policy includes nine principles that guide EPA's relationship with Indian tribes and implementation of its programs on Indian reservations.

Federally Recognized Tribes: Tribes with whom the federal government maintains an official relationship, usually established by treaty, congressional legislation, or executive order.

Indian Country: In broad terms, Indian country is all the land under the supervision of the U.S. government that has been set aside primarily for the use of Indians. All land within the limits of any Indian reservation under the jurisdiction of the U.S. government, notwithstanding the issuance of any patent, and including rights-of-ways running through the reservation.

Jurisdiction: The legal power a government has to govern its people and territory.

Litigation: Legal contest carried out through the judicial process.

Public Participation: When the public is informed of a federal action, and the federal government solicits citizen input before making a decision.

Reservation: Lands reserved for tribal use.

Self-Determination: Decision-making control over one's own affairs and the policies that affect one's life. This is also the name of the federal government's policy toward Indian nations, beginning in 1978.

Sovereign: Supreme in power or authority.

Sovereignty: The status, dominion, rule or power of a sovereign. Tribes have the power to make and enforce laws for their tribe and reservation, and to establish courts and other forums for resolution of disputes. Tribal sovereignty is not absolute, but rather is subject to certain limits resulting from the subordination of the tribes to the United States.

Tradition: Cultural beliefs and customs handed down from ancestors.

Traditional Cultural Properties (TCP's): Beliefs or practices of a people tied to land or water, in conjunction with religious beliefs and/or practices.

Treaty: Formal, legally binding contract between two sovereign nations; an agreement between two or more nations, relating to peace, alliance, trade, etc.

Tribe: A group of individuals bound together by ancestry, kinship, languages, culture, and political authority.

Trust: Property held by one person for the benefit of another.

Trust Doctrine: This is rooted in the treaties between Indian tribes and the U.S. government where Indian land was ceded to the government, under treaties, in exchange for protection of the land and tribal rights. In this doctrine, the U.S. government holds title to Indian land in trust for the beneficial use of Indian tribes and their members. This includes other protection, including protection of the Indians' sovereign rights.

Village: Term used to denote a community of Alaskan natives.